Practical Storage Area Networking

Practical Storage Area Networking

Dan Pollack

✦ Addison-Wesley

Boston • San Francisco • New York • Toronto • Montreal
London • Munich • Paris • Madrid
Capetown • Sydney • Tokyo • Singapore • Mexico City

The publisher offers discounts on this book when ordered in quantity for bulk purchases and special sales. For more information, please contact:

U.S. Corporate and Government Sales
(800) 382-3419
corpsales@pearsontechgroup.com

For sales outside of the U.S., please contact:

International Sales
(317) 581-3793
international@pearsontechgroup.com

Visit Addison-Wesley on the Web: www.awprofessional.com

Library of Congress Cataloging-in-Publication Data
Pollack, Daniel, 1970–
    Practical storage area networking / Daniel Pollack.
      p. cm.
    Includes bibliographical references and index.
    ISBN 0-201-75041-4 (pbk. : alk. paper)
     1. Storage area networks (Computer networks) I. Title.

  TK5105.86 .P65 2003
  004.6--dc21

                        2002074787

ISBN 0-201-75041-4

Text printed on recycled paper

1 2 3 4 5 6 7 8 9 10—MA—0605040302

First printing, September 2002

For my parents, who always knew I could,

For my friends, who forced me to get started,

And for my wife, who was patient while I did.

CONTENTS

LIST OF FIGURES

PREFACE

This book is for systems administrators, storage administrators, and anyone else who has been given the difficult and unglamorous task of ensuring that data can be stored and retrieved consistently, for any application, in their environment. Anyone with intermediate knowledge of storage devices and how they are integrated into applications and systems can use the information in this book to build a storage area network, or SAN. SANs have become a major technology for deploying storage, and one can find extensive discussion about their merits and limitations. However, very little has been written about the actual nuts and bolts of SAN building and operating. This book describes what I have done when implementing my own SANs, with the goal of enabling builders of storage systems to progress from thinking about SANs to doing them.

The examples of SAN building I offer here are not intended to be complete recipes, because each environment is unique. Instead, I will illustrate a number of good practices that help bridge the gap between the concept for a SAN and the physical deployment of a SAN. My hope is that these practices will create a framework for SAN builders to refer to when a SAN is the solution to the problem their particular requirements present.

The book pays particular attention to the assessment of input/output (I/O) behaviors in host systems, storage devices, and applications. This focus is the starting point for the SAN designs discussed throughout the book. I/O assessment is particularly important because it helps set expectations and parameters for an initial SAN design.

The consistent discussions of several typical SANs throughout the book take the reader through the planning, assessment, design, deployment, and operation phases of these SANs. By structuring a SAN project logically and dividing it into distinct phases, readers can reduce the amount of work involved in building a SAN.

Applying the methods in this book to your own environment should be very straightforward. Examples are given for each SAN implementation phase discussed, so that you can apply the information to most SAN projects. The book also examines the future of SANs, to enable SAN designers and implementers to plan for and accommodate new or expected SAN features without completely reengineering existing SANs.

ACKNOWLEDGMENTS

I would like to thank all of the people who helped me with this project from start to finish. I could not have done any of this without Karen Gettman of Addison-Wesley. Karen first got me excited about writing the book and then provided guidance while helping me make progress during the whole process. Thanks also to Emily Frey for making the details painless. John Fuller helped make the communications simpler. Don Lafferty's editing and suggestions helped make the book much clearer and better organized. I'd like to thank the reviewers for all of their help, suggestions, and constructive comments, as well as their valuable time.

The great folks I work with at America Online Inc. also deserve thanks. Geoff Salinger's encouragement and confidence in my abilities to build our first SANs were an enormous help. Thanks to my manager, Anne Grenade, for her patience with every new SAN. Scott McClung and Eric Wall provided an invaluable sounding board for technical topics. The employees of SGI Inc., Brocade Communications Systems Inc., and EMC Corp. who support America Online have also been great.

Practical Storage Area Networking

1

SAN DEFINITIONS, CONCEPTS, AND COMPONENTS

1.1 What Is a SAN?

A storage area network (SAN) is a network of devices that connect host systems to storage devices. A SAN's fabric is its specific infrastructure, encompassing any devices that connect to host systems, storage devices, or each other. For example, Fibre Channel switches and the optical cables that connect them are typical components of SAN fabrics. The fabric provides the connectivity between host systems and storage endpoints.

A SAN takes the one-to-one relationship between the host-system port and the storage-device port and creates a one-to-many relationship for both host and storage ports at the edge of the SAN. The flexible one-to-many relationship between any particular edge port and all of the other edge ports on the SAN allows any number of connections to be made. All of the available paths between a particular pair of endpoints can be used to transfer data across a SAN.

The multipath nature of the SAN provides configuration flexibility, availability, and scalability.

- ***Flexibility.*** Software configuration eliminates or reduces the need to rerun cable when storage allocations or layouts change.

- ***Availability.*** Multiple paths protect against path failures between host systems and storage devices.

- ***Scalability.*** Load balancing across multiple SAN paths provides better systems predictability by smoothing and increasing overall utilization. Also, connecting devices together without direct cabling creates a fanning-out effect for I/O ports that allows many more devices to be connected together than direct attachments allow.

The effective combination of the features of SANs will improve storage deployment operations for most systems and applications. Improved scalability and availability of the storage subsystem will also benefit almost all applications in some way.

1.2 NAS versus SAN

Network-attached storage (NAS) is often mentioned as an alternative to storage area networks. NAS and SANs do share some qualities, and there is some overlap in their potential application. But there are important differences as well, so it is useful to take a quick look at NAS and SAN together.

The main advantages of SANs are bandwidth, performance, and efficiency of access to storage.

- ***Bandwidth.*** SANs are based on 1Gbps Fibre Channel links today, and the speed of SANs will continue to increase as Fibre Channel performance improves. NAS performance will also improve as IP networking speeds increase, but the timelines for Fibre Channel and Ethernet are almost the same. Fibre Channel also has additional bandwidth to accommodate protocol overhead, so SAN links run at full rated speed.[1] In comparison, the most common NAS devices use 100Mbps Ethernet, which is one-tenth the speed of Fibre Channel.

- ***Performance.*** Even if 1Gbps Ethernet is used to access NAS devices, there is still more protocol overhead for TCP/IP. Ethernet and TCP/IP frame header information is more than twice the size of Fibre Channel header information, and Fibre Channel frames are larger than Ethernet frames. The larger Fibre Channel frames allow more data to be transmitted between every acknowledgment, improving useful data throughput. TCP/IP must also be processed by the host operating system at a higher level than block I/O traffic. This means more work for the operating system, which reduces throughput. The Fibre Channel SAN data-transfer bandwidth always outperforms the gigabit Ethernet NAS data-transfer bandwidth.

- ***Access to storage.*** SANs provide a flexible connection infrastructure for host systems to allocate storage device access. NAS devices have a similar flexible infrastructure for access to data. The SAN access method becomes more rigid once a storage entity has been allocated to a host system. This allocation creates a one-to-one relationship for the storage entity with potentially several physical paths for data access, but all paths are known at allocation time.

  All NAS data accesses involve communication with the NAS server or metadata engine. The checking of metadata can have performance and access-contention issues. SAN storage devices simply deliver blocks to systems that request them. NAS devices first check the metadata attributes of the requested data and then perform a local file system operation in order to deliver the data.

---

1. 1Gbps Fibre Channel actually runs at 1.0625 Gbps. See the Fibre Channel Physical and Signaling Interface draft at ftp://ftp.t11.org/t11/member/fc/ph/fcph_43.pdf for more information.

The total data transferred by a NAS device may be smaller than the same request from a SAN storage device. However, the overhead required to find out exactly which small chunk of data needs to be sent delays the transfer enough in most cases to make it slower than sending the whole data block.

NAS systems may eventually converge with SAN systems so that they both can use the same physical infrastructure and can perform the same tasks. SANs will need to become as manageable as NAS devices. NAS devices will require performance improvements and better data access methods for greater stability. Because NAS and SAN differ in significant ways, their differences should be compared carefully when deciding what storage system to deploy for a specific application. When a SAN is a good fit for a project, the implementation can be approached using the procedures in this book.

1.3 SAN Hardware

SAN hardware components make up the complete SAN infrastructure and provide the platforms for the SAN software features. The devices used to build SANs include the following:

- Logical endpoints: host system host bus adapters (HBAs) and storage devices

- Networking devices: Fibre Channel switches and hubs, and Fibre Channel-to-parallel SCSI bridges

- Application devices

- Gateway devices

Figure 1.1 shows some typical SAN components and how they can be connected.

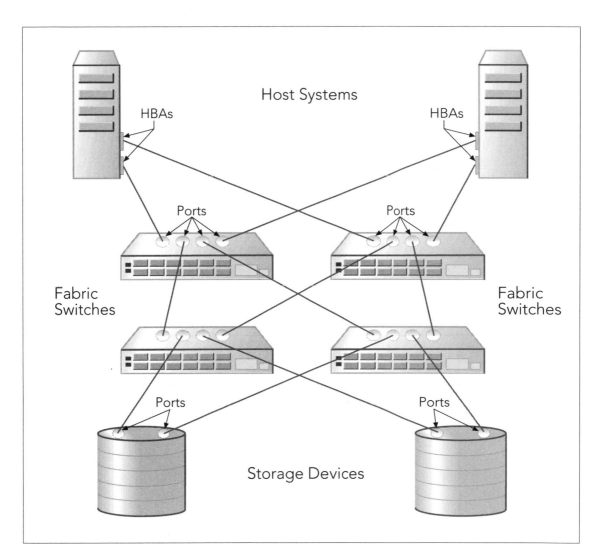

FIGURE 1.1

SAN components

Logical Endpoints

HBAs define one of the logical endpoints on the SAN because they provide the I/O channel that a host system uses to connect to the devices on the SAN. HBAs connect the internal I/O bus of a host system to a storage system I/O channel. When HBAs are used on a SAN instead of direct attachment to storage devices, they are configured to perform proper SAN attachment and log in to the SAN fabric.

Storage devices are the other logical endpoints in a SAN. Most SAN storage devices are intelligent disk array devices. Intelligent disk array devices contain groups of disks connected to a processor that provides:

- External access to the disks

- Data protection such as RAID

- Performance enhancements with a high-speed RAM cache

- Any additional services such as storage allocation

Any SAN-aware storage device can attach physically and log in to the SAN fabric in order to provide storage and storage services to host systems. These storage devices provide the storage space and data transfer performance engine for the SAN.

Storage devices can be used in several ways on a SAN, depending on the performance and storage requirements of applications. Different storage devices will have different data protection and performance enhancement methods, which create a wide range of possible choices for use on a SAN.

Network Devices

Fibre Channel switches create dynamic connections from incoming to outgoing ports within the switch device. A Fibre Channel switch allows multiple full-link-speed data transfers to occur within the switch without any one data transfer stealing resources from any other. The bandwidth of a Fibre Channel switch is the speed of any single link multiplied by up to half the total number of ports in the device. This limit is due to the fact that all incoming ports require outgoing ports to make a complete connection. For example, in a sixteen-port Fibre Channel switch, the maximum bandwidth through the device is 800MBps because eight ports at most can be incoming while eight others must be outgoing.

Fibre Channel hubs repeat incoming traffic to all connected devices. All hub ports share a single common bus for all I/O traffic, so the ports are limited to the performance of the single bus. Hubs also broadcast incoming traffic to all ports, so that all attached devices receive traffic that is meant for only one of the attached devices. Hubs also broadcast errors, making them prone to cascade failures. When all attached devices receive an error and attempt to simultaneously correct the error, even more errors occur. Hubs can still be used for fanout of more costly switch ports, if careful planning of the layout is done to reduce the potential for transmission of errors that impact host systems.

Fibre Channel to parallel SCSI bridges connect legacy storage devices (devices that do not have a Fibre Channel interface) to a SAN. Bridges separate the SCSI protocol traffic from the parallel SCSI physical interconnect in order to pass the data traffic to a SAN. The connection of existing devices to a SAN with bridges is very useful if old data must be preserved or if the data must be accessed temporarily while a migration to a SAN is underway.

Bridges can also be used to connect a device to a SAN when the device has not been built with a Fibre Channel interface. Tape drives and robots in tape-changing devices are examples of devices that may not have a Fibre Channel interface. Some of these devices are now being built with Fibre Channel interfaces for convenience, but they may still be connected to a SAN with a bridge if a Fibre Channel interface is unavailable.

Application Devices

Occasionally an application using a SAN requires a storage service that is not provided by a storage or fabric device. In this case there are several SAN application devices available that meet the requirement. SAN application devices can be simple host systems loaded with special-purpose SAN software or SAN-aware special-purpose devices with a specific task such as virtualization of storage or data caching. Virtualization is discussed in detail later in this book, but for now, it can be thought of as the abstraction of the physical attributes of any single storage device, or group of storage devices, into a logical pool of storage resources such as total storage capacity or data bandwidth. SAN application devices generally increase performance or utilization of the SAN with a feature enhancement that augments the abilities of storage devices to store and transfer data. An example of a SAN application device is a cache engine through which a host system accesses a storage device. A cache engine improves performance by increasing the cache size of the storage device beyond what can be installed in the device itself.

Gateway Devices

SAN gateways are the newest type of hardware devices available for SANs. SAN gateways are being developed with many different transports, to provide as many connectivity choices as possible. These devices allow SANs to span long distances while performing a translation of the SAN Fibre Channel transport to an IP transport. For example, a SAN that currently supports direct backups over the SAN fabric has to contain the backup devices as well as the storage devices. Eventually, using a SAN gateway, the backup devices can be moved to their own separate SAN and shared between several other SANs instead of just the host systems on a single SAN. Gateway devices will also allow separate SANs to be connected for limited data-transfer purposes without requiring the connected SANs to be merged. This separation of SANs is preferable to simply zoning or masking devices apart from each other in the same SAN, and then adding and removing devices from zones or unmasking and remasking when necessary. Zoning or masking of devices creates the logical connectivity between SAN endpoints that either creates or removes device separation. Separation is preferable because it reduces fabric reconfigurations that can cause instability in a SAN.

1.4 SAN Software

Several types of software work together to provide data access from endpoint to endpoint. The software components of a SAN include these:

- Operating systems for Fibre Channel fabric devices, hosts, and storage devices

- Drivers and firmware for HBAs

- Managers for SANs and storage devices

All of these software components then work together using standard methods to transfer data.

Operating Systems

Fibre Channel–device operating systems reside on active Fibre Channel devices such as switches. The switch operating system manages all of the features of the switch hardware and provides the configuration interface for those features. The switch operating system also provides monitoring and event output that can be used by built-in tools or external management systems.

Host system operating systems may need to support a different access method for SAN storage compared to direct-attached storage. Host system operating systems that are SAN-aware can address devices on the SAN fabric. The support for SAN-attached storage allows applications to use SAN storage simply by addressing a device using its SAN identifier in the device tree instead of a directly attached device identifier.

Storage device operating systems reside in the processors of intelligent disk arrays. Storage device operating systems control the functioning of the array and provide an interface for any control of the array that is required, such as logical unit number (LUN) creation and allocation or data-protection-scheme changes. Monitoring of the array is also done by means of an interface to the storage device operating system. This enables the storage device to send event messages about itself directly, without having to connect to a host system for event forwarding.

HBA Drivers and Firmware

HBA drivers and firmware combine to deliver the HBA's features and functionality. The HBA firmware allows the HBA to connect and log in to the SAN. A SAN login procedure consists of two steps:

1. The HBA identifies the type of connection it should make with a device.

2. The HBA exchanges operating parameter information with the device, if it is a compatible SAN-fabric device.

The HBA driver also connects the host operating system to the HBA's firmware features. These features allow the host system to use the HBA for device connectivity.

All HBA software will eventually implement a standard API being developed by the Storage Network Industry Association (SNIA)[2] for monitoring and configuration. This standard will allow all devices

---

2. http://www.snia.org/

aware of the API to configure and monitor HBAs, which will simplify management of these devices.

Managers

SAN managers are rapidly evolving toward aiding in the management and monitoring of SANs. To configure SAN components, SAN managers aggregate many device-specific management methods and SAN management standards. For example, to create a complete SAN control console, SAN managers may combine:

- APIs for switch device control

- HBA APIs from SNIA

- Host system command line control tools for storage arrays

- Host system volume manager command line tools

The methods and their specific combination depend on the devices the SAN manager supports.

SAN management software may also provide an event console for notification of SAN component problems. SAN managers can be a key component for storage deployment and assessment in a SAN by providing a unified interface for the monitoring and managing of the large number of devices installed in a SAN.

Storage device managers control and configure storage devices. Configuration interfaces may not be available to SAN managers, so device-specific tools must be used in that case. Storage device managers are also used to control features of the device that SAN managers cannot access or do not currently include. For example, storage device replication mechanisms are features that should be controlled by the storage device manager instead of the SAN manager tools. The storage device control changes required in a failure situation may be too complex for an external tool to manage properly.

SAN Applications

SAN applications are used to access data stored on the SAN, as opposed to manager software, which is used to control and monitor the SAN itself. Figure 1.2 shows some typical SAN applications and where they run in a SAN. SAN applications, running on a host system or network device, enable more efficient data storage and storage device management, because the application itself is SAN-aware and can make use of the networked nature of the storage and host systems. SAN applications are currently available for data movement and sharing. Services currently provided by a more traditional IP network mechanism are being migrated to the SAN. For example, backups, other data archival applications, and concurrent data access applications are all being implemented using SAN applications.

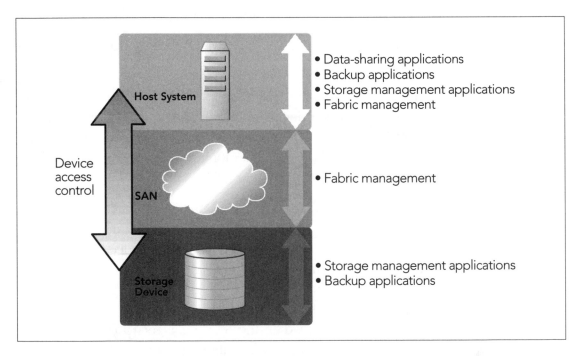

FIGURE 1.2

SAN-aware applications

1.5 Typical SANs

The purpose of designing and building a SAN is to support applications storage requirements and storage growth needs while improving the management and flexibility of deployed storage. With that in mind, it is helpful to examine a few typical SANs. Later chapters of the book discuss the implementations of these SANs in detail.

NAS Replacement

NAS replacement SANs improve NAS application performance. Currently there are two common uses for NAS: data sharing and centralized backup. Data-sharing applications use a network device to control concurrent access to a file system for many client systems. Backup systems use a master system on a network to act as a funnel for backup of data to storage devices attached to the master system. Both types of NAS applications can benefit from the performance increase a SAN can potentially provide. These applications profit from more deterministic data transfers on the data sharing or backup SAN. The gain comes from more predictable data transfer times, which facilitate work scheduling with less padded job windows.

Storage Consolidation

Storage consolidation SANs improve storage allocation. Storage consolidation is the grouping of storage devices into a shared pool so that storage can be allocated more efficiently and more rapidly. Host systems then allocate only the amount they need from the shared pool instead of an entire storage device. Storage consolidation SANs reduce wasted storage resources and allow for better planning of storage deployments.

Capacity Planning

Capacity-planning SANs facilitate a quicker reaction to application needs. Storage devices can be deployed in a shared pool without the specific known allocations associated with a storage consolidation SAN. As application storage needs change, the capacity-planning SAN can allocate storage and manage growth without requiring major changes to host system architectures. Capacity-planning SANs reduce the downtime related to storage upgrades, improve storage utilization, and simplify rapid application deployments.

New Project

New project SANs provide a flexible storage deployment method to meet the needs of a project with unknowns related to the project's storage and performance. When an application has been defined but the exact requirements may change as the application is deployed, a SAN is an effective way to deploy storage for a new project. A SAN for a new project will reduce the impact of required reconfigurations due to unforeseen application behaviors and allow for any overconfiguration to be addressed when the application has stabilized.

Experimental

Experimental SANs can also be used for investigations of the technologies and devices that are used to build SANs. An experimental SAN enables full investigations of SAN use, deployment, and management workload. Many SANs deployed today are evaluated in production with very little idea of the actual behaviors and characteristics that can be expected from the systems and applications. Experimental SANs can be used to discover how devices and software will work together in the SAN environment without the pressure of servicing the storage requirements of a critical system.

When deploying applications on a SAN, it is important to evaluate the fit of the application with SAN storage. SANs can improve the storage attributes of applications if they are well matched to the strengths of a SAN. Careful evaluation and design are very important to make sure applications and SANs will work well together.

1.6 Implementing a SAN Project

To avoid being overwhelmed by the details of SAN deployment, it is important to examine a SAN with respect to some basic constraints. The structure or type of the SAN, the expected behaviors and performance of the systems that will use the SAN, and the components selected to construct the SAN are good starting points to gather information.

The structure or type of SAN you want to deploy will help set expectations for the applications that will use the SAN. An examination of this aspect of a SAN may also uncover new uses or interesting operational modes for the applications.

The performance analysis for the SAN design will create a baseline for comparison between expectations and observations of a running SAN. The performance analysis of applications and systems is also beneficial when diagnosing problems, because there are known system behaviors that can be used as reference for normal operating conditions.

Selecting components for SANs can be a difficult process without complete knowledge of the options. The extremely large number of components can also be problematic. Developing ways to limit the number of possible components used and to use only components of known quality will improve the chances for success when undertaking a project like a SAN deployment.

1.7 Summary

In this chapter, we have presented a high-level overview of SAN components and classified the kinds of typical SAN projects that are undertaken in the real world. With this framework in mind, we can proceed to discuss the steps involved in every SAN project. The first step, the planning phase, is the topic of the next chapter.

2

SAN PROJECT SELECTION

This chapter breaks a SAN project into small pieces so that we can analyze and design each part. The topics discussed in this chapter include the general types of SANs, I/O performance assessment, and SAN application evaluation. The fundamental concepts and descriptions presented here provide the basis for references to SAN components and characteristics for design and deployment throughout the rest of the book.

2.1 Storage Solutions

Deployments of storage for systems include three common solutions.

- ***Direct attachment to the host system.*** Direct-attached storage (DAS) is a resource dedicated to the connecting system. The connectivity of DAS is the main deployment constraint. Limited sharing of a device may be possible with large storage devices used in a direct-attached mode if there is sufficient connectivity and if multiple storage partitions are possible within the unit.

- ***Access through an IP network, as in NAS.*** NAS storage is a shared resource that uses IP networking and file system sharing protocols such as Network File System (NFS) or Common Internet File System (CIFS) for access. The primary constraint of NAS is the performance loss associated with using TCP/IP as the data transport.

  NFS provides transparent remote access to shared file systems across networks. NFS is designed to be independent of machine, operating system, network architecture, and transport protocol.[1] CIFS is an enhanced version of Microsoft's cross-platform Server Message Block (SMB) protocol, the native file-sharing protocol in the Windows family of operating systems. CIFS is widely available on many NAS platforms.[2] NFS and CIFS enable file sharing and storage access via IP networks and differ only by the types of client systems they commonly support.

  The number of systems that can use a NAS device for storage is limited only by the ability of the NAS device to service requests and the throughput of the network between the device and its client systems. NAS enables the sharing of the same file systems among multiple client systems, which creates significant scalability for systems with mostly read-only workloads such as static Web site content.

- ***Access through a dedicated storage network, as in SANs.*** Although the dedicated network can be an IP network, this is not necessarily the case for SANs. SAN storage is accessed through a fabric that offers both flexibility in its connectivity options and high performance for data throughput. Many servers can access SAN storage, similar to NAS, but SANs have much lower overhead and a dedicated storage fabric for higher performance, usually based on Fibre Channel. SANs combine

---

1. See RFC 1813 at http://www.cis.ohio-state.edu/cs/Services/rfc/rfc.html for complete NFS details.

2. See the MSDN online magazine at http://www.microsoft.com/mind/defaulttop.asp?page=/mind/1196/cifs.htm for complete CIFS details.

TABLE 2.1.   Storage Access Characteristics

	Direct-Attached Storage	Network-Attached Storage	Storage Area Network
Flexibility	Poor	Good	Good
Performance	Excellent	Fair	Very Good
Connectivity	Poor	Good	Good

the configuration and deployment flexibility of NAS with the high performance data throughput usually associated with DAS. Table 2.1 shows the characteristics of storage access types.

2.2 Potential SAN Projects (Likely Choices)

Begin a SAN project by identifying the storage problems it needs to solve and the type of SAN that best delivers the solution. SAN projects solve one of a few general problems. There are specific SAN types that apply to these general problems, and selection of the proper type at the start of the project simplifies the solution.

Typical Problems

The three most common problems that SANs address are these:

1. ***Increasing utilization through consolidation.*** Consolidation of resources reduces the amount of wasted capacity in an environment and is a common goal of SANs.

2. ***Data or resource sharing.*** SANs enable a finer level of control over resource allocation. SANs for data or resource sharing implement features of NAS on a dedicated fabric for storage traffic. SAN fabrics provide increased performance and stability for data transfers while maintaining resource flexibility.

3. ***Capacity planning.*** SAN configuration flexibility creates a significant head start for deploying systems and storage with a limited amount of information. Final project specifications can be accommodated with logical configuration changes to a SAN rather than having to wait for a complete project specification before beginning work.

Identifying a SAN Type

The general types of applications for a SAN are the following:

- Storage consolidation

- NAS replacement

- New project

- Capacity planning

- Experimental

These types describe almost all SAN projects and enable an initial characterization of the design, analysis, and management requirements.

Knowing the SAN type enables you to examine the application that will use the SAN in the most appropriate way. This analysis allows you to develop a good SAN design focused on the particular behaviors of the target application.

An application examination may also reveal that a SAN is the wrong choice for your application I/O subsystem. Very extreme application performance requirements make SAN storage a poor choice. Extreme performance usually requires very rigid configurations with extremely deterministic behaviors. At this point SANs do not have the control or monitoring levels that extremely high performance applications require. The application analysis may also reveal that there is little benefit to having a more flexible storage system. Systems with little growth expectation and with known, unchanging resource requirements will probably see little benefit from a SAN.

STORAGE CONSOLIDATION SAN

One of the most common storage problems occurs when there is too much free space on one host while another host has none. The storage consolidation SAN seeks to eliminate this problem by allocating free storage resources from a shared pool to any host that requires storage resources at any time. Figure 2.1 shows a typical storage consolidation SAN.

In addition, storage consolidation SANs can do the following:

- Provide services to multiple hosts

- Support heterogeneous host and storage devices

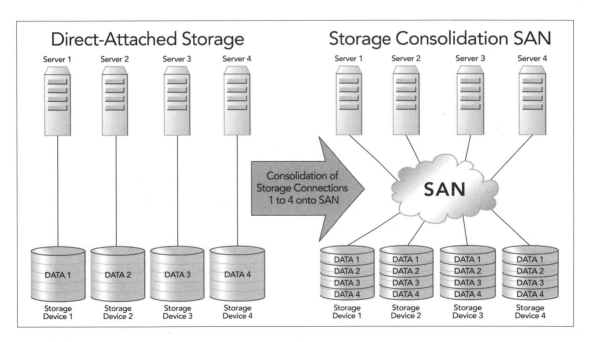

FIGURE 2.1

Direct-attached storage versus storage consolidation

- Support host application failover

- Improve data transfer

Consolidation SANs are common in large organizations attempting to utilize more fully their available storage resources.

NAS REPLACEMENT SAN

NAS replacement SANs improve data transfer bandwidth and create resource flexibility that network-accessed storage cannot provide. The flexibility of device allocation that a SAN provides can be of significant value to a NAS replacement SAN used for backups. NAS replacement SANs can either take the place of file-sharing systems that use IP networks, such as NFS and CIFS, or provide an alternate path for data transfers, as in the case of network-based backup systems. In NAS replacement SANs, the fabric takes the place of the traditional network or provides a second network that provides enhanced services and more deterministic or higher performance.

In addition, NAS replacement SANs can do the following:

- Provide concurrent access to storage devices

- Allow the exchange of storage devices between systems

- Simplify data accesses across systems

Figure 2.2 shows a typical NAS replacement SAN.

NEW PROJECT SAN

A new project SAN takes advantage of a specific SAN feature. A project with specific SAN needs but no legacy system to compare with or analyze can be optimized to take advantage of the target SAN feature. This type is likely to be the easiest to design and build.

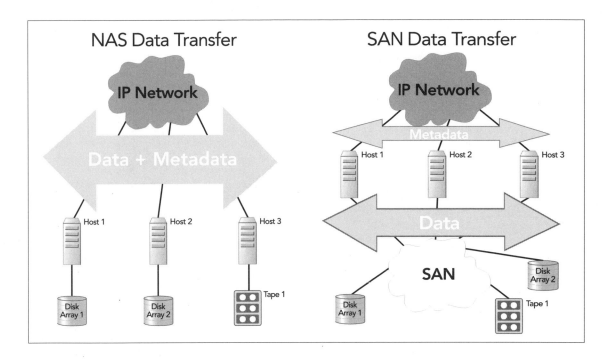

FIGURE 2.2

Generic NAS replacement with a SAN

Typical SAN features for a new project SAN include multipath port fanout and SAN data transfer methods. Multipath port fanout for large storage devices with low physical connection port counts enables connectivity with large numbers of hosts. For example, a four-port storage device can be directly attached to only two hosts with redundant paths for the storage. In a SAN configuration, the number of hosts with redundant paths to the storage device ports can greatly increase within the performance requirements of the application and the fabric. SAN-specific I/O features such as multipath I/O or device sharing can enhance the new application environment and can be configured to get the most out of the SAN. Multipath I/O provides better availability for data because multiple access paths to the same data eliminate single points of failure in the I/O infrastructure. Figure 2.3 shows a new project SAN.

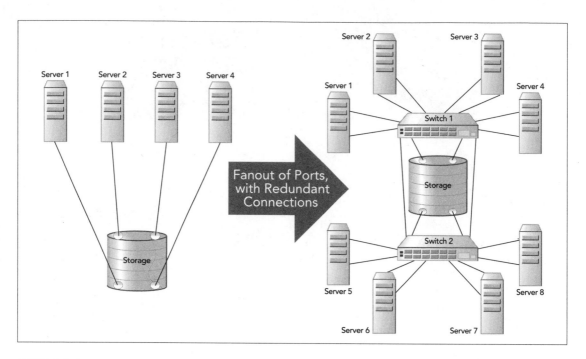

FIGURE 2.3

SAN for a new project. Note port fanout, improved I/O channel redundancy, and increased server count.

CAPACITY-PLANNING SAN

Capacity-planning SANs facilitate deployments. When rapid deployment of systems is necessary and little or no forecasting is available, then planning new infrastructure to accommodate new applications with the most flexible resource allocation possible is extremely beneficial. All of the hardware and most of the software can be integrated well in advance of anticipated project needs. Anticipating project needs leaves only the final configuration to be accomplished at deployment. Flexible infrastructure also eases redeployment of host systems from one application to another. Deploying more capacity-planning SANs in a specific environment reduces the uncertainty in the SAN configurations over time. Figure 2.4 shows a capacity-planning SAN.

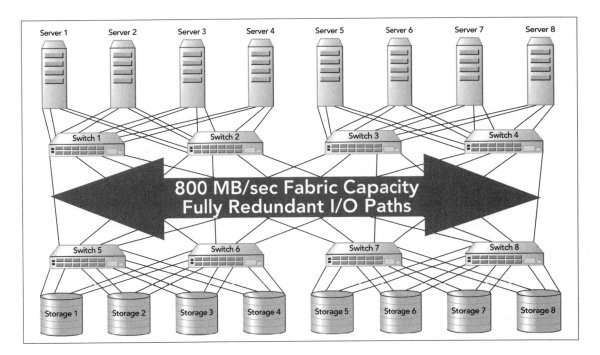

FIGURE 2.4

Capacity-planning SAN

EXPERIMENTAL SAN

An experimental SAN can be a useful tool for refining all other potential uses of SANs when the time comes to build and deploy a production SAN. It can be extremely helpful to have a low-risk environment when evaluating SAN behaviors with new hardware, software, zoning methods, or storage device configurations. Experimental SANs can also facilitate the evaluation of the performance of desired configurations, without having to make changes to critical on-line systems.

2.3 Understanding Trade-offs

The flexibility and storage services available on SANs can require trade-offs in terms of four factors:

- Performance

- Configuration

- Management

- Availability

The design choices made when implementing the SAN must take all of these trade-offs into account. Eventually, implementers will need to make these choices clear to users of the applications hosted on the SAN.

Performance

The performance behaviors changed by design compromises are the most difficult to determine. Design compromises that accommodate imperfect SAN components, such as components with fewer I/O channels than desired, must be made and can worsen performance and availability. It is difficult to evaluate the effects of the design compromises because of interactions between devices that may be unpredictable in the design.

Performance differences between SAN and non-SAN storage can be assessed partially through the use of I/O models and partially through application testing. Unfortunately, neither method is guaranteed to indicate exactly what the application will do. Because the I/O and application models are simplified representations of the behaviors in the systems being examined, they are not exact. They are close enough to be useful tools for SAN design and evaluation. Later in this chapter, we will see what to use to evaluate I/O behaviors; in Chapter 3, we look at detailed examples of I/O assessment and modeling.

Once the application is running on the SAN, changes may be needed to address the performance issues that were not discovered through evaluation with I/O models. The models help to provide validation after deployment by confirming design integrity through comparison of observed behaviors on the implemented SAN with expectations from the models. If there are large differences between expectations and measured results, implementers need to investigate why the differences exist. The outcome of the examination determines whether the model needs refining or the SAN needs repairing.

Configuration

Configuration of storage and host systems for use in a SAN varies widely between SAN implementations. Device naming and presentation on the host platform usually differ from DAS, requiring a new set of naming standards for your environment. SAN LUN names often include references to the world-wide name (WWN) of the port or device that the LUN resides in. This means that SAN devices must be addressed differently than directly attached devices, and new abstractions that indicate a device is accessed through a SAN are helpful. SAN device name differences are specific to the operating system being used.

Configuration also requires some additional tools that provide device allocation, protection, and monitoring. To manage device allocation, use LUN-masking or device-zoning tools. LUN masking provides access controls to storage systems at the LUN level. Accesses to LUNs in storage devices by HBAs in host systems are controlled by LUN masking. Zoning groups storage devices at the I/O port level. Zones create groups of ports that are visible to each other and restricted from ports not in the zone. Ports are not exclusive to a zone and may be in more than one zone at a time. Both of these features are important for data protection and fault isolation in a SAN.

Management

Management of SANs requires an additional layer of monitoring that DAS does not have. Hosts and storage devices must be managed, but fabric devices also must be managed. There are several fabric management methods, including the following:

- Simple Network Management Protocol (SNMP)

- Storage industry standards from several different groups, including the SNIA HBA API

- Proprietary, vendor-specific tools, such as the Web server–based management tools built into most Fibre Channel switches

Most devices that make up a fabric have more than one management interface, so implementers can pick the ones that best meet their needs and fit their environments.

Availability

Availability of storage accessed through a SAN can be affected by the components chosen, the I/O layout, and the monitoring systems. For example, hot-swap components and redundant I/O paths improve the availability of the SAN. The more features that are implemented to make the SAN better able to react to failures of any sort, the more available the SAN will be. The increased SAN availability translates directly to better application availability.

Summary

When designing a SAN, performance boundaries, configuration methods, and management methods should be documented as completely as possible in the beginning in order to clarify design goals. This process also helps to set better expectations for application behavior. System delivery times will also be easier to estimate when deployed using the SAN. Setting expectations at the beginning facilitates agreement on final design decisions and selection of baseline metrics.

2.4 I/O Requirements by SAN Type

A reasonable guess about the I/O behavior of an application, and therefore the storage subsystem, goes a long way toward formally assessing the application. Based on the type of SAN and the target application, a number of useful things can be inferred before formal assessment of the application.

Storage Consolidation SAN I/O

A storage consolidation SAN should not have extreme performance requirements. However, use of consolidation tends to indicate a requirement to service varied workloads, and these workloads have the potential to cause contention somewhere in the SAN. The contended-for resource can be one of many, including these:

- Storage space

- Storage device bandwidth

- I/O channel bandwidth

- HBA I/O operations per second (IOPS)

It is best to size a storage consolidation SAN with as much overhead as possible for the resource that is expected to be limited.

Some perfectly reasonable guesses can be made with respect to what the limited resource will be if the systems for consolidation are known at design time. For example, on-line transaction processing (OLTP) database servers are likely to run out of IOPS performance before anything else. The likely locations for the bottleneck will be storage device CPUs, HBAs, or packet-forwarding saturation in a switch.

Another example involves systems that perform business-reporting jobs. Such systems require good bandwidth and large amounts of storage space to process the data sets associated with business intelligence. In a SAN, the most likely shortage for these systems is bandwidth. For example, business intelligence systems sort and analyze very large amounts of data as quickly as possible, so they work in large chunks as fast as possible.

Space shortages will affect all systems that grow over time. A good assessment of usage over time prevents shortages in even the most rapidly growing systems. The I/O modeling section of Chapter 3 contains an in-depth examination of the I/O behaviors of a storage consolidation SAN.

NAS Replacement SAN I/O

NAS replacement SANs will likely target improved performance of the existing system. Figure 2.2 (see page 23) shows generally how a SAN replaces a NAS environment. The metadata continues to move across the IP network while the bulk of the data moves across the SAN. SAN services can use the metadata services in the same way that NAS services such as NFS use the metadata. In addition, the NAS replacement SAN usually uses the same software that the NAS system uses to implement metadata traffic exchange. SANs gain an advantage by splitting the I/O into two distinct streams of low latency metadata and high bandwidth data.

I/O performance differs between NAS replacement SANs for file sharing and for backups. NAS replacement SANs generally need good data streaming performance. But file-sharing SANs require low latency because shared files are likely to be used interactively and may change frequently. Frequent updates require rapid metadata updates to the shared files to maintain performance. If the metadata updates slow down, then so will the accesses to files, because all files must have their metadata examined before any new operation can be performed.

On the other hand, NAS replacement SANs for backup devices may run out of bandwidth in the SAN before encountering any other bottleneck. A bandwidth shortfall is likely in the case of backup SANs, because backups transfer large amounts of data in large chunks from one point to another as quickly as possible.

New Project SAN I/O

SANs designed from the ground up for new projects may have the fewest bottlenecks and performance problems because they can be designed to anticipate the specific requirements of the new project. Anticipating application needs and defining performance expectations facilitates SAN design and specification, assuming that the requirements are within achievable values. For example, design of a high-performance data warehouse staging SAN can include the extreme bandwidth requirements of that workload. Design of user authentication systems with high peak usage rates can include the extreme IOPS demands.

Capacity-Planning SAN I/O

The performance parameters of a capacity-planning SAN must meet the performance needs of the anticipated applications. Capacity planning for a SAN that supports data warehouse applications must include a design that accommodates high bandwidth, because large I/Os and few IOPS are common in that environment. Capacity-planning SANs for OLTP systems will have less available storage space but more features that accommodate high IOPS loads, such as large RAM caches. High-rate OLTP systems try to keep the data sets small to prevent scans of large data sets from slowing the system. The large RAM caches in storage devices are used to reduce the access times to the most common data from milliseconds in the case of a disk access to nanoseconds for RAM access.

Experimental SAN I/O

Develop experimental SAN designs to meet the goal of an investigation. For example, build bottlenecks into the SAN with expected threshold values and applications, or run I/O load models to exploit bottlenecks. Constraining IOPS in the experimental SAN while running OLTP processes with large numbers of small I/Os allows a thorough investigation of SAN performance when there is a shortfall of IOPS performance. Experiments on software and hardware modes of behavior can be extremely helpful when finally moving on to the deployment of production SANs for everyday use. These experiments include the running of a standard I/O load on the experimental SAN and then changing the performance of the hardware or software by modifying tunable parameters or in some other way. For example, hardware can be evaluated under failure conditions by removing a hot-swappable component in order to simulate a failure.

2.5 Application I/O

With a clear idea of SAN type, it is time to undertake a thorough application analysis with respect to likely bottleneck areas. In order, the areas to investigate are the following:

1. Bandwidth requirements

2. IOPS performance

3. Typical I/O size

4. I/O use patterns during operation

5. Storage usage

Use host system tools or application documentation and tools to assess these parameters. All operating systems come with built-in tools that provide information about the performance and usage of the critical subsystems such as I/O, memory, and CPU. The picture of assessed performance becomes the basis for design decisions in the SAN.

Bandwidth

A measurement of aggregate utilization of all bandwidth is a good place to start. Additional measurements can examine individual I/O channel bandwidth performance, if necessary. These measurements look for the distribution of application data across all available I/O devices. Uneven distribution of the data suggests modifications of the application itself in order to enable better data distribution. If the application cannot be changed, then the SAN design must allow for uneven distribution. In this case, the design needs to accommodate additional hardware that improves the performance of the I/O subsystem.

Generally, tools that output information on I/O operations performance can output information on bandwidth as well. The UNIX *sar* utility is one such tool. Figure 2.5 shows an example of the output from the *sar* utility. The figure shows the information that *sar* provides concerning the I/O behavior of the individual disk devices attached to the host system. The device column identifies the individual device names. This information is useful when attempting to pinpoint a specific device. The column labeled "blks/s" gives the total bandwidth usage per second of a device; multiplying that number by the block size in bytes will convert it to the more common MB/s. See Chapter 3 for specific examples of the use of system tools such as *sar* for I/O measurement. See Table 2.2 (on page 36) for additional information.

```
                          Sum this column            Sum this column
                           for total IOPS           for total bandwidth
 hostname % sar -d 5 5000

 IRIX64 host  6.5 01200532 IP27      07/06/00

 22:31:21    device %busy  avque  r+w/s  blks/s   w/s  wblks/s  avwait  avserv
 22:31:26    dks0d1    1    1.0    0.6      5     0.6     5      0.0     16.7
             dks0d2    1    1.0    0.6      5     0.6     5      0.0     16.7
             dks0d3    1    1.0    0.4     10     0.4    10      0.0     15.0
             dks0d4    1    1.0    0.4     10     0.4    10      0.0     15.0
             dks0d5    2    1.2    1.6     32     1.4    29      1.2     13.8
             dks0d6    2    1.3    1.4     29     1.4    29      2.9     11.4
             dks1d6    0    0.0    0.0      0     0.0     0      0.0      0.0
```

FIGURE 2.5

UNIX *sar* output

Bandwidth requirements drive the selection of the SAN connectivity devices. All of the connectivity devices need to be capable of very high throughput if the application on the SAN requires high bandwidth usage.

IOPS

IOPS requirements commonly drive storage device selection because most hosts with above average IOPS requirements have multiple channels to intelligent storage systems. The column labeled "r+w/s" in Figure 2.5 gives the combined read-and-write IOPS performance of each device per second. Storage systems are typically the limiting factor for IOPS. IOPS performance is closely tied to the ultimate performance of the storage devices used to store data. The host systems create the demand for IOPS, and the I/O channels transport the IOPS that the storage devices must service.

See Table 2.2 (on page 36) for typical IOPS performance ranges for individual I/O channels and host system aggregates.

I/O Size

An application's typical I/O size can affect the tuning of the SAN. The typical or working I/O size of an application is the size of the most common I/O operations in bytes. To find the working I/O size, read the application documentation or with less certainty investigate the application with system tools. Knowing the typical I/O size facilitates configuration of I/O system parameters for peak possible performance.

For example, system parameters can include data stripe size and the number of devices to stripe. Volume managers or storage devices that implement RAID features use data stripes to distribute data across multiple devices. In contrast, a concatenated group of devices spills data from one device to another as each device becomes full. In the case of a concatenated volume, a storage device CPU or volume manager lays out the volume on one disk until the end of the device is reached before writing data to the next device. This effect is similar to glasses of water filling and then overflowing into other glasses below. Striped devices use small chunks of data on each device in a group to create more uniform usage of the devices in the group.

All RAID levels for data protection or performance use striped data allocation except RAID 1, which is usually combined with RAID 0 to provide disk striping. To improve performance, it is possible to tune storage system or volume stripe size to the I/O size of an application by making the stripe size a multiple of the application I/O size. If an application performs tasks that typically generate sixteen 8KB I/Os at a time, then a good stripe size may be 128KB. This setting causes each application task to be serviced by a different device in the group, assuming good data alignment between the requests and the layout of the data.

TABLE 2.2.   I/O Performance Ranges

	Host IOPS	Channel IOPS	Host Bandwidth	Channel Bandwidth
Low	0–3000	0–500	0–50 MB/s	0–10 MB/s
Average	3000–20000	500–1500	50–200 MB/s	10–40 MB/s
High	>20000	1500–10000	200+ MB/s	40–100 MB/s

I/O Patterns

Identifying I/O patterns facilitates decisions regarding which type of I/O to favor. Application I/O patterns include these:

- ***The read-I/O-to-write-I/O ratio.*** Applications that have a high read-I/O-to-write-I/O ratio, with a large random I/O percentage, require a SAN design with good IOPS performance.

- ***The percentage of sequential access I/O an application performs.*** Streaming applications with a large percentage of sequential I/O require high-bandwidth performance.

- ***The percentage of random access I/O an application performs.***

Table 2.2 shows typical I/O performance ranges for I/O channels as well as entire host systems with multiple I/O channels.

An example of a host system with high bandwidth usage in Table 2.2 is one that either has a single channel above 40MB/s or a host system aggregate bandwidth of more than 200MB/s. This host system requires one or more high-performance I/O channels, such as Fibre Channel interfaces, to maintain this performance.

Storage Requirements

Determining storage space requirements should be one of the less difficult assessment tasks, but it is still an important one. Too much space means idle storage, which is a waste of resources. Too little space is difficult to manage and requires immediate expansion at deployment.

Storage usage and planning is highly specific to individual environments, but a good rule of thumb sizes the SAN to accommodate two acquisition cycles worth of data growth. If it takes three months to get a new storage device, then the SAN should have enough space to contain six months of application growth without any additions. This allocation allows the application to continue to run without incident while dealing with unforeseen problems in the acquisition of new storage.

2.6 Additional Project Requirements

Now that we have a good feel for the basic parameters of a SAN with respect to how the SAN compares to existing I/O subsystems, it is time to specify additional requirements, including these:

- SAN-based file sharing

- Multipath I/O, with or without failover

- SAN data transfer

- SAN data replication

File Sharing

SAN-based file sharing requires design decisions concerning SAN deployment beyond the I/O performance requirements. Anticipation of homogeneous or heterogeneous clients, and the number of them, helps to determine the implementation of a file-sharing solution. Performance targets for shared-file writes and reads and their relationship affects the implementation as well. Features of the SAN-aware file-sharing solution such as server failover also need to be taken into account.

Read-and-write I/O performance is a significant factor in the selection of a SAN file-sharing system. SAN file-sharing I/O performance determines whether the requirements of the application using SAN file sharing can be serviced. The performance of a SAN file-sharing solution must be evaluated in the SAN environment where it will run, to ensure that expected and actual performance agree.

Heterogeneous clients reduce the number of options available to implementers for the choice of a SAN file-sharing server because there are very few that support more than one client type. A SAN file-sharing server allows for easier addition of new file-sharing clients or client types in the future. The standard IP networks required to support file sharing are also important. Any IP connectivity can be used for the network component of SAN file-sharing systems. While the IP networks are only lightly used when performing file sharing over a SAN, they are still a required part of the system and should have the lowest possible communications latency in order to facilitate rapid metadata updates.

Availability of the file-sharing servers needs to be set at an achievable level for the sharing software and the chosen hardware. If the shared files require above-average availability, then the system requires support for highly available or fault-tolerant server hardware and software. This selection will likely have an effect on the homogeneous versus heterogeneous client decision, because there are few SAN file-sharing solutions that currently support both high availability and more than one or two client types.

Multipath I/O

Many SANs allow host systems to take advantage of the many-to-many nature of the SAN fabric and provide multiple access paths to storage devices from those host systems, that is, multipath I/O. Multipath I/O increases the availability of host-system access to storage in the event of a channel failure anywhere in the SAN.

If the SAN uses multipath I/O, then the multipath solution has several configuration options, depending on the host systems and storage devices. These configuration options provide one of the following:

- Channel failover only, which provides an inactive backup I/O channel that can become active in the event of a primary I/O channel failure, such as a cable break.

- Round-robin I/O distributes I/O requests over all of the available I/O channels to a storage device one after another. This crude form of I/O load balancing is susceptible to aliasing problems caused by uneven I/O distributions that may cause one channel to overload while others are relatively unused.

- Dynamic load-balancing multipath I/O evaluates the I/O load on each channel to a storage device and then chooses the best path for each I/O request. I/O load is assessed with software added to the host system I/O subsystem. The software implements a policy that is favorable to application performance, such as IOPS performance being favored for an OLTP system.

Not all host systems or storage devices can support all multipath I/O configuration options, but all fabric-aware devices should support at least one.

Data Transfer

SAN data transfer can be used to an application's advantage by providing generally higher performance and a more deterministic method for moving data files from point to point than an IP network. SAN data transfer uses the SAN to move a complete data set, such as a file, instead of its usual mode of operation, which is simply to transfer data blocks. SAN data transfer requires a higher level of host system or application awareness on the SAN, which is achieved with SAN application software. An IP network can achieve the same speeds as a Fibre Channel–based SAN, but the IP network requires a gigabit Ethernet infrastructure and still has greater protocol overhead.

If the SAN supports data transfer, the transfer takes place in one of two general ways:

- Using the fabric directly for dedicated file transfer

- Running IP traffic on the SAN fabric

Either option can be deployed based on the devices chosen for the SAN. The dedicated system will be a proprietary solution. Proprietary solutions require a specific server and client or peer-to-peer system installed on all of the systems that will use the SAN for data transfer. The IP-over-fabric solution can be more general because it uses known IP services, but due to IP networking requirements, the solution requires additional configuration of network ranges, name service, and fabric HBA device drivers.

Data Replication

Features available on either the host systems or the storage devices can accomplish data replication.

HOST-BASED DATA REPLICATION

Host system software options exist for data replication on some host types, but not all. For example, many UNIX operating systems lack the ability to replicate data internally within the host system or externally to another host system. Some operating systems, but not all, have the ability to run third-party products that provide this feature. All host system types should support data replication in some way. This requirement is most common for disaster recovery solutions, but it can be used for other applications, such as application data snapshots, for increased scalability and availability.

The host-based data replication options that are available do not require special storage. However, they do require host software processing, either continuously or at least while replication is taking place.

Host-based data replication requires the host system to transfer data between storage devices. Figure 2.6 shows the basic components of a host system data replication process. A host process copies the incoming data to separate storage devices. Either copy of the data can then be accessed independently by the host system. This process is different from mirroring, in which the two copies of the data are not independently accessible. The requirement that the hosts transfer the data to both storage devices usually makes it difficult to reallocate the replicate storage device regularly for operational use on a separate host system.

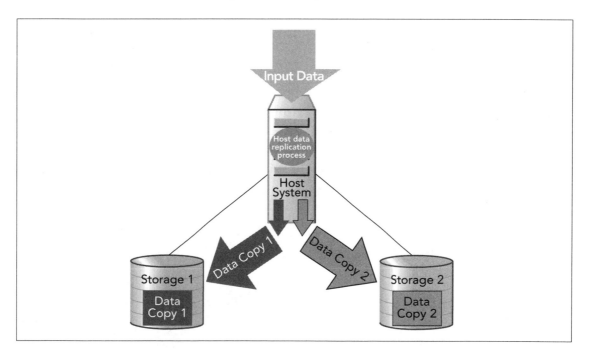

FIGURE 2.6

Host-based data replication

Host-based data replication options make good scalability tools for use on the same host system. Scalability for an application can be achieved if additional data sets are available for the application and if the application is primarily read-only. Under these conditions, multiple read-only applications, each with its own copy of the data set, can be run on the same host system. This increases the through-put of the application by servicing more requests and increases uti-lization of the host system.

STORAGE-BASED DATA REPLICATION

Data replication done by the storage device requires little or no host processing, but it is available on only some storage devices. Very sophisticated enterprise-class storage devices are currently the only devices that have replication features built-in.

Figure 2.7 shows the basic components of a storage device data replication process. The host system stores the incoming data, and then a process in the storage device forwards a copy to another stor-age device. Because no host system processing is involved, the repli-cate storage device does not require a direct connection to the source host. This makes attaching the replicate storage device to a different host simpler, and allows storage-based data replication to be used for disaster recovery and replication of batch-processing applications that can be run from data snapshots. The CPUs within storage devices create snapshots by copying data from one set of internal devices to another, or by making a copy of the pointers to data and preserving any changed data by copying that data when a change is made to the original.

Storage-based data replication is likely to appear on more storage devices as time goes on and as features from high-end enterprise-class storage devices migrate to lower end commodity storage devices.

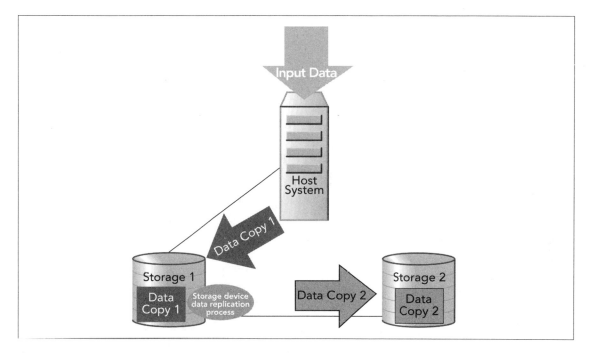

FIGURE 2.7

Storage device–based data replication

CHOOSING A DATA REPLICATION SOLUTION

The application and the expected use of the replicated data determine the type of replication you should choose. The higher the application performance requirement, the more likely that storage device–based replication will be necessary, due to its use of a secondary path for data transfer. Host-based replication has a multiplying effect on network bandwidth utilization. Replicated data will most likely be received from the network and then replicated back out onto the network. This behavior can exceed the capacity of the network adapter if the host IP network cannot support the increased bandwidth demands.

2.7 Summary

This chapter has covered the general rules for selecting a SAN storage solution and the general requirements for each solution. Now that the SAN project has been categorized in general terms, we can proceed with an analysis of the specific behaviors of the application and the SAN, with a slant toward the likely constraints expected from the SAN type being implemented. All of the I/O behaviors and configuration possibilities can be examined to meet the needs of the SAN and the applications using it.

3

PROJECT MODELING

Project modeling is done as an investigation of the design constraints of a project. In a SAN project, the I/O behaviors of the host systems and applications that will use the SAN are examined for extremes and trends. A good project model takes into account the complete range of tasks the SAN is expected to perform and is based on existing systems or reasonable estimates. A good project model does not have to take a long time to complete, provided assumptions can be made about the expected results to limit the amount of examination required. Models allow the designer to verify the resulting SAN behaviors without the risk of moving critical applications and host systems to the SAN. Start modeling your project with assessments of storage and I/O workload requirements.

3.1 Storage Requirements

Storage requirements can be determined from general rules and knowledge of the target SAN type.

General Rules for Sizing Storage

The expected data set size, or the data set size plus the expected growth of the data set if it already exists, determines the storage requirements. Application users, developers, and database administrators should have an idea of the type of data being stored and characteristic sizes, so they are good sources of sizing information. In a new application, if the typical record size in a database or the size of commonly stored data for an application can be determined, then simply multiply the size by the total expected starting number of records to determine the total amount of storage. If growth can be predicted on the basis of the number of users or the number of records, then storage can be sized for expected growth as well. A last resort for sizing information can simply be a guess based on general information about the new application.

Requirements by SAN Type

Depending on the type of SAN being implemented, assumptions about the amount of storage required can eliminate much of the storage size analysis.

STORAGE CONSOLIDATION

To determine a storage consolidation SAN's requirements, look at the target host systems, add up all the storage in use on the host systems, and add the growth rates of the data on those host systems. A storage consolidation SAN more efficiently accommodates the storage space growth rates of the host systems because all storage space in the SAN is available to all host systems.

NAS REPLACEMENT

A NAS replacement is similar to a storage consolidation SAN. To determine the amount of storage needed, add up all the storage space in use on the existing NAS and look at the expected growth rate of the data stored on the NAS systems.

NAS replacement SANs that implement tape backup require a different storage sizing method due to the unlimited total storage of removable media devices. Size a NAS replacement SAN for tape backup by determining the number of tape drives required to service the backup workload. The number of tape drives depends on all of the following:

- The number of concurrent backups

- The amount of data to be backed up

- The amount of data each tape will store

- The amount of time available for system backups

A complete discussion of backup system sizing would be a digression here; there are several good books on this topic. As a simple rule of thumb, use one tape drive for each concurrently backed up file system. Unless the data sets are small, avoid backing up data from multiple sources onto a single tape. Resource contention and possible restore conflicts can occur if multiple backups for different host systems are on the same tape.

CAPACITY PLANNING

For capacity-planning SANs, determine the size of storage by looking at the data set sizes of systems likely to use the SAN. A capacity-planning SAN that supports data warehouse extraction, transformation, and load (ETL) processing has greater storage requirements than a capacity-planning SAN that supports OLTP. This difference reflects the generally smaller overall sizes of high-performance OLTP applications. To estimate a good storage size, look at the typical storage size and the growth requirements of the target systems. If a given system requires 200GB of storage today and doubles in size every six months, and another like it is deployed every six months as well, then a reasonable sizing estimate for a six-month capacity-planning solution is 800GB.

EXPERIMENTAL

Experimental SANs require little or no analysis of storage sizing. Because the purpose is pure experiment, the typical size of a system from your environment makes the best test case. If the experimental SAN's storage size is too small, the investigations cannot yield enough information. If the storage size is too large, there is obvious waste.

NEW PROJECT

When attempting to size a SAN for a new project with little or no relation to any existing system, it is important to find out as much as possible about the new application. Investigation of the expected record size and the number of records goes a long way toward determining the required storage space. System and application overhead requires an additional 10 to 25 percent of space. The expected growth of the application data is also important when planning for system growth.

3.2 I/O Size Requirements

To discover the characteristic I/O size, gather information on data access. If possible, also gather information on data access patterns with respect to read-and-write ratios. If the access patterns cannot be discovered by looking at application specifics—such as logs, in the case of Web servers, or transactions, in the case of OLTP servers—then gather the data from host system tools. On UNIX systems use the *sar* command to look at the raw disk I/O behavior. On Windows

NT systems, use the *perfmon* command. This data will shed some light on typical I/O sizes and the access patterns.

The raw data can be processed to show some additional interesting I/O behaviors. With a few simple rules of thumb applied to the raw data and the processed data, the analysis can provide all of the information necessary for the design of the SAN. This process yields a set of boundaries for the SAN design goals with respect to the application. At completion, the analysis provides requirements for maximum bandwidth, maximum IOPS, and the amount of storage space. The next two sections take a detailed look at the examination of I/O workload on host systems.

With definite requirements in hand, hardware and software can be selected and integrated to meet specific application needs. Evaluation follows to determine whether the SAN meets expectations or requires any additional changes.

3.3 I/O Assessment and Analysis Tools

The best way to look at I/O behaviors and performance is to look at system tools on the hosts that run the applications. An examination using system tools provides a top-down view of the I/O subsystem from the host system's perspective. A higher level view of the I/O behaviors can sometimes be extracted from an application, such as a relational database management system (RDBMS), but not all applications have the ability to report this data. Further, there is no consistent way to extract the data for the applications that report I/O statistics.

Because of this inconsistency and because system tools tend to be more consistent in their availability and data set measurement, it is best to start with the system tools themselves. The system tools provide a distilled version of the application I/O behavior at the device level. Any additional application-level device abstractions are lost, but the raw I/O behaviors will still show through in the analysis.

It is possible to perform an analysis of the I/O system from the storage device point of view in a bottom-up fashion. This method does not have the problems of an application-level analysis because of the common availability of useful statistics on almost all intelligent storage devices. Information gathering takes place with device-specific methods because standards for the contents of the data set and the data extraction method are not quite complete.[1] New storage device management standards will make data gathering from storage devices more complete and consistent, so that all devices can provide the same basic utilization and performance data. Implementation is in various stages depending on the hardware and software vendors, the products in use, and the chosen device management method.

In general, put off device analysis until the host system analysis is complete. The storage device analysis has greater depth and narrower scope, and it requires more effort to perform. Delaying this analysis enables a more focused approach on the storage devices, whose greater amount of storage-specific I/O data can easily swamp the investigator.

A few simple scripts written in Perl or a shell language can quickly examine UNIX hosts that have the *sar* utility. *sar* is a very useful tool to use, available on almost all UNIX operating system variants. The *sar* data set and output are quite consistent from UNIX to UNIX. The data available from the Windows NT *perfmon* command can also be processed fairly easily from its logged format.

A quick look at the *sar* man page on your UNIX host system will provide details on the timing and amount of data gathered. On most

---

1. The Fibre Alliance is continually updating the Fibre Channel MIB for SNMP, and the SNIA has developed a complete storage management and information standard, the Common Information Model, based on the Distributed Management Task Force Web-Based Enterprise Management.

UNIX host systems, the data is the past week's-worth of system data. A simple spreadsheet analysis of the data can provide information on maximum system bandwidth and IOPS. The analysis can also show patterns of usage throughout a day or several days. Once the script is run on each host system, the collected data can be examined and combined with data collected from other host systems, if necessary, to provide a complete snapshot of the host system's workload.

The get_io.sh script in Example 3.1 performs two functions:

1. It gathers bandwidth and IOPS data from a host system.

2. It outputs data files from *sar* input data for analysis in a spreadsheet.

The analysis of the data set gathered from the script is performed by putting the comma-separated-value output files of each data type (bandwidth or IOPS) for each day assessed into a spreadsheet. The data can then be graphed versus time in order to visualize the I/O behaviors of the host system under evaluation in the modes of bandwidth, IOPS, and I/O size. The visualization of the data reveals some significant I/O parameters for the SAN design, such as maximum bandwidth utilization, maximum IOPS utilization, workload windows, workload consistency, and characteristic I/O sizes. Additional mathematical analysis may be of use if the visualization of the data provides poor insight into the I/O behaviors of the analyzed host system, but usually this is not required.

The fairly simple script in Example 3.1 takes data collected by the *sar* utility and creates twenty-minute aggregated data points of bandwidth and IOPS from the host system perspective on all I/O channels combined. See Figure 3.3 (on page 61, top) for an example of the output of the get_io.sh script. The two sets of output files from the script can also be combined to find out the typical I/O size of the application being examined over these intervals.

EXAMPLE 3.1.   The get_io.sh shell script

```
#!/bin/sh
# get_io.sh
# Gather aggregate bandwidth and IOPS data from a host's sar data files
# Gather bandwidth data from sar archives
day=1
for sarfile in `ls /var/adm/sa/sa[0-2]*`
do
  shour=0
  ehour=0
  min=0
  while [ $shour -le 23 ]
  do
    ehour=`expr $shour + 1`
    interval=0
    # Divide each hour into 3 parts because the data is in 20-minute
    # intervals
    while [ $interval -le 2 ]
    do
      case "$interval" in
        0)
        blocks=0
        sum=0
        # Extract the data from a sar archive file and
        # sum the blks/s column
        for blocks in `sar -d -f $sarfile -s $shour:00:00 -e
        $shour:20:30 | egrep -v "IRIX|sun4|HP-UX|AIX|,|^[0-2]"
        | awk '{print $5}'`
        do
          sum=`expr $sum + $blocks`
        done
        # Clean up any old temp files, then compute bandwidth
        rm -f /usr/tmp/bcfile
        echo $sum " / 2 / 1024" >> /usr/tmp/bcfile
        echo quit >> /usr/tmp/bcfile
        bw=`bc -l /usr/tmp/bcfile`
        # Store the bandwidth result in a csv file
        echo $bw >> /usr/tmp/bw_$day.csv
        # Report the bandwidth result
```

EXAMPLE 3.1 (*continued*).   The get_io.sh shell script

```
echo "Bandwidth is" $bw "MBps"
;;

1)
blocks=0
sum=0
for blocks in `sar -d -f $sarfile -s $shour:20:00 -e
$shour:40:30 | egrep -v "IRIX|sun4|HP-UX|AIX|,|^[0-2]"
| awk '{print $5}'`
do
  sum=`expr $sum + $blocks`
done
rm -f /usr/tmp/bcfile
echo $sum " / 2 / 1024" >> /usr/tmp/bcfile
echo quit >> /usr/tmp/bcfile

bw=`bc -l /usr/tmp/bcfile`
echo $bw >> /usr/tmp/bw_$day.csv
echo "Bandwidth is" $bw "MBps"
;;

2)
if [ $shour -eq 23 ]
then
  break
fi
blocks=0
sum=0
for blocks in `sar -d -f $sarfile -s $shour:40:00 -e
$ehour:00:30 | egrep -v "IRIX|sun4|HP-UX|AIX|,|^[0-2]"
| awk '{print $5}'`
do
  sum=`expr $sum + $blocks`
done
rm -f /usr/tmp/bcfile
echo $sum " / 2 / 1024" >> /usr/tmp/bcfile
echo quit >> /usr/tmp/bcfile
```

EXAMPLE 3.1 (*continued*).   The get_io.sh shell script

```
          bw=`bc -l /usr/tmp/bcfile`
          echo $bw >> /usr/tmp/bw_$day.csv
          echo "Bandwidth is" $bw "MBps"
          ;;

      esac
    interval=`expr $interval + 1`
    done
    shour=`expr $shour + 1`
  done
  day=`expr $day + 1`
done

# Gather IOPS data from sar archives
day=1
rm -f /usr/tmp/bcfile
for sarfile in `ls /var/adm/sa/sa[0-2]*`
do
  shour=0
  ehour=0
  min=0
  while [ $shour -le 23 ]
  do
    ehour=`expr $shour + 1`
    interval=0
    while [ $interval -le 2 ]
    do
      case "$interval" in
        0)
        ios=0
        sum=0
        # Extract the data from a sar archive file and
        # sum the r+w/s column
        for ios in `sar -d -f $sarfile -s $shour:00:00 -e
        $shour:20:30 | egrep -v "IRIX|sun4|HP-UX|AIX|,|^[0-2]"
        | awk '{print $4}'`
        do
         echo $ios "+ \\" >> /usr/tmp/bcfile
```

EXAMPLE 3.1 (*continued*). The get_io.sh shell script

```
      done
    echo 0 >> /usr/tmp/bcfile
  echo quit >> /usr/tmp/bcfile
    # Compute the IOPS
  iops=`bc -l /usr/tmp/bcfile`
      # Store the result in a csv file
      echo $iops >> /usr/tmp/ios_$day.csv
      # Report the result
      echo "IOPS are" $iops
    # Clean up any old temp files
  rm -f /usr/tmp/bcfile
      ;;

      1)
      ios=0
      sum=0
      for ios in `sar -d -f $sarfile -s $shour:20:00 -e
      $shour:40:30 | egrep -v "IRIX|sun4|HP-UX|AIX|,|^[0-2]"
    | awk '{print $4}'`
      do
        echo $ios "+ \\" >> /usr/tmp/bcfile
      done
  echo 0 >> /usr/tmp/bcfile
  echo quit >> /usr/tmp/bcfile
  iops=`bc -l /usr/tmp/bcfile`
      echo $iops >> /usr/tmp/ios_$day.csv
      echo "IOPS are" $iops
  rm -f /usr/tmp/bcfile
      ;;

      2)
      if [ $shour -eq 23 ]
      then
        break
      fi
      ios=0
      sum=0
      for ios in `sar -d -f $sarfile -s $shour:40:00 -e
```

EXAMPLE 3.1 (continued).   The get_io.sh shell script

```
            $ehour:00:30 | egrep -v "IRIX|sun4|HP-UX|AIX|,|^[0-2]"
            | awk '{print $4}'`
            do
              echo $ios "+ \\" >> /usr/tmp/bcfile
            done
        echo 0 >> /usr/tmp/bcfile
        echo quit >> /usr/tmp/bcfile
        iops=`bc -l /usr/tmp/bcfile`
            echo $iops >> /usr/tmp/ios_$day.csv
            echo "IOPS are" $iops
        rm -f /usr/tmp/bcfile
            ;;


        esac
        interval=`expr $interval + 1`
        done
        shour=`expr $shour + 1`
      done
      day=`expr $day + 1`
done
```

The get_iosize.pl script in Example 3.2 takes pairs of bandwidth and IOPS output files from the script in Example 3.1 and uses the simple equation

I/O size = Bandwidth (KB/s) / IOPS

to generate the typical I/O size over the same intervals.

The output of this script will add a bit more detail to the analysis of the application and host system. See Figure 3.3 (on page 61, bottom) for an example of the output from the get_iosize.pl script. The graphic analysis of the data shows patterns and anomalies. The more regular the patterns look in the graphical analysis in terms of IOPS, bandwidth, and I/O size, the more likely it is that the conclusions drawn from the patterns will be useful. Less consistent graphs indicate

EXAMPLE 3.2.   The get_iosize.pl shell script

```perl
#!/usr/local/bin/perl
#
# get_iosize.pl
# Find the characteristic I/O size from the output of get_io.sh script
$i=1;
while ( $i <= 7 ) {
    # Open the result file for output from this script
    open (OUTFH, ">>/usr/tmp/iosize_$i") || die "Can't open file, $!\n";
    # Open and read the bandwidth and IOPS output csv file pair
    open (BWFH, "/usr/tmp/bw_$i") || die "Can't open file, $!\n";
    @bwinfo=<BWFH>;
    close (BWFH);
    open (IOPSFH, "/usr/tmp/ios_$i") || die "Can't open file, $!\n";
    @iopinfo=<IOPSFH>;
    close (IOPSFH);
    # Make sure the number of data collection intervals
    # in each file matches or quit
    if ( $#bwinfo != $#iopinfo) {
        printf "The files for day $i don't match. Exiting\n";
        exit;
    }
    $j=0;
    # Divide the bandwidth in KBytes by the number of IOPS
    # to get the I/O size
    while ( $j <= $#bwinfo) {
        if ( @iopinfo[$j] != 0) {
            $iosize = $bwinfo[$j] * 1024 / $iopinfo[$j];
            } else {
            $iosize = 0;
            }
        # Report the I/O size result and record it in an output file.
        printf "Typical IO size is $iosize\n";
        printf OUTFH "$iosize\n";
        $j++;
    }
    close (OUTFH);
    $i++;
}
```

more variable system usage, making the sizing task more difficult. Pattern uncertainties can lead to overconfiguration and waste of resources in the SAN design.

3.4 Analyzing Key Application I/O Characteristics

With some data in hand, it is time to look at several examples of application complexes in order to determine the characteristics of the host systems and applications. A comparison of each application complex with the expected SAN type shows the configurations that work best and the settings that need to be applied.

When looking at the output of the I/O assessment tools used to gather data, apply local environment rules of thumb to the analysis. If the analysis of the data seems to indicate an oddity, then the local behaviors of the users or supporting systems will also need to be evaluated. For example, an oddity may be a moving peak usage time period on a system that runs the same workload every day. Additional analysis can help explain the unexpected behaviors and facilitate a more accurate sizing of the design. For example, a data warehouse batch job that starts daily at different times due to variable size of the input data set is one situation in which a moving peak usage time may be observed.

NAS Replacement SAN for an NFS Server

In the first system for examination, a SAN replaces a NAS server running NFS, as shown in Figure 3.1. The NAS server provides archived business intelligence in order to avoid retrieval of tape backups for recently processed data sets. Retrieval of data sets occurs in the case of processing errors, processing failures, or additional processing needs. The server holds several weeks of data, and the data set sizes are gradually growing. Specifically, the NAS server has been growing at a rate of approximately 100 percent every twelve months. To find

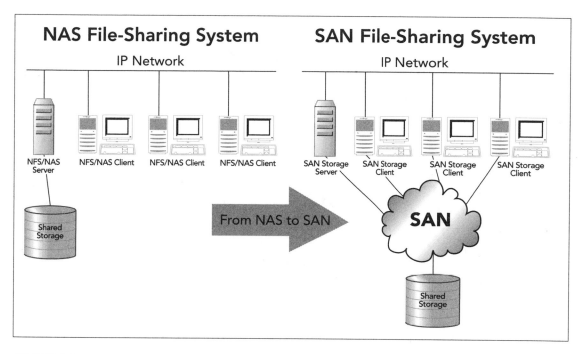

FIGURE 3.1

NAS replacement SAN for file sharing

the growth rate, determine how much storage has been added over the past twelve months and make a few quick inquiries about expected uses over the next twelve months. Now we understand the storage requirements for the SAN system.

Using the output of the scripts in Examples 3.1 and 3.2, it is possible to create several graphs of the data. The graphs show a few interesting characteristics of the NFS server. Figure 3.2 shows the bandwidth usage for the entire system over the period of a week.[2] This aggregate display of bandwidth shows that the application does not consume much bandwidth. Only a fast SCSI or slower device interconnect has trouble with the peak bandwidth of the system. This fact

---

2. A week may not be enough data, so further data gathering may be required. In this case, one week is enough.

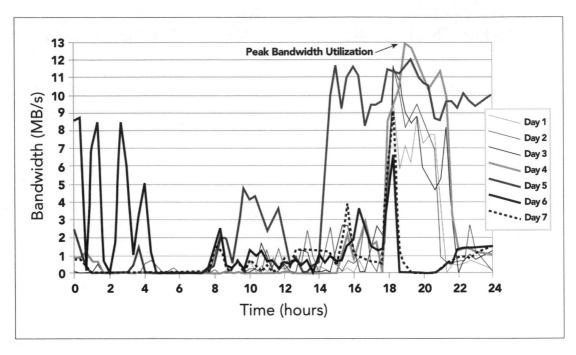

FIGURE 3.2

NFS server bandwidth versus time

gives a great deal of flexibility when choosing the SAN infrastructure and topology, because Fibre Channel or any other interconnect can easily handle this bandwidth.

Figure 3.3 shows the performance of the NAS server. The first graph in Figure 3.3 shows that the system will have an IOPS load close to, but not exceeding, the lower region of the IOPS performance scale for a single HBA, which Table 2.2 shows to be 500 IOPS (see page 36). This load allows for flexibility in the SAN configuration because the configuration requires only one HBA to service the IOPS and bandwidth load. Obviously other factors such as multipath I/O will affect the final number of HBAs used, but performance is not an issue based on the likely choices of hardware and the application requirements.

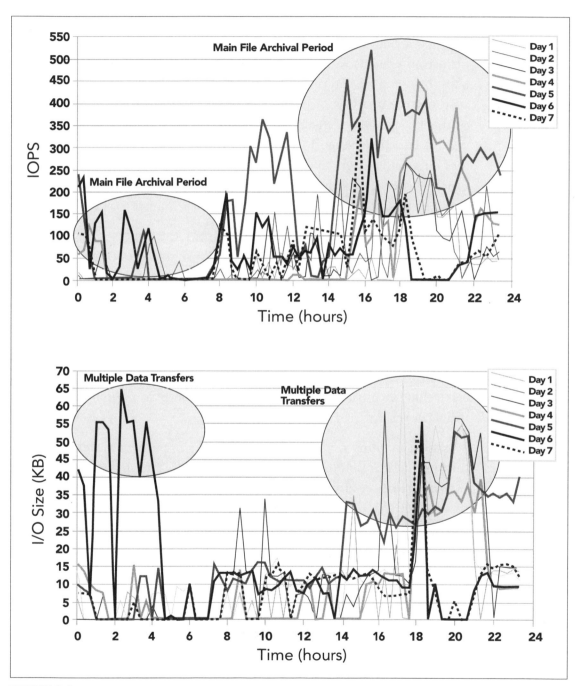

FIGURE 3.3

Top: NFS server IOPS versus time. *Bottom:* NFS server I/O size versus time

The second graph in Figure 3.3 shows I/O size with respect to time for the period of a week. The I/O size graph shows that the system performs I/O in the 12KB to 16KB size characteristic of NFSv2. Peak I/O sizes can be larger than the NFS transfer size, because this is a systemwide analysis; the larger I/O sizes are approximate multiples of the typical NFS transfer size. Based on knowledge of the application, it can be assumed that during these times, multiple data transfers cause the aggregate I/O size to appear larger than expected. A quick inspection of the system processes during one of these periods shows that the assumption of multiple data transfers is correct.

No real oddities have been found from the analysis of the NAS server, and the parameters for the design have been obtained. Before defining the I/O model created to test the SAN design, a few more system types should be examined.

Storage Consolidation of a Data Warehouse (ETL) System

Data warehouse (ETL) staging systems make good examples of systems that are appropriate for storage consolidation. Figure 3.4 shows the systems.

The host systems perform daily ETL tasks for a data warehouse system in a large customer service organization. The data provides general information about groups of customers in order to help provide more focused services to individuals in those groups. The storage devices are initially empty and then filled as projects arise. ETL systems perform mostly memory-intensive data transformation tasks. The I/O load on these systems consists mostly of file writes of the transformed data and data transfers to and from the host system.

STORAGE SPACE REQUIREMENTS

The amount of storage required for these systems is the sum of the following factors:

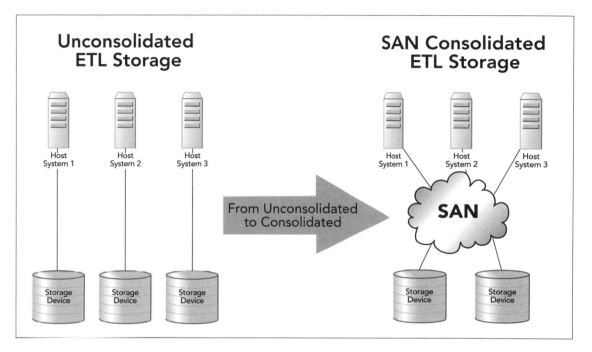

FIGURE 3.4

Storage consolidation SAN for data warehouse

- The space to receive the raw business intelligence files

- The scratch work space for file transformation

- The output area for the processed files

- The archive area (if any)

To gather this information, look at the existing host systems.

The storage growth of the consolidated host systems is the sum of these two requirements:

- The amount of storage needed to contain data sets as they grow

- The amount of storage needed to accommodate additional data transformation output by any new processes

There is an additional potential reduction in excess storage from redeployment of unused storage using the shared pool in the SAN.

An examination of the three data warehouse staging hosts shows that the amount of storage grows about 1TB every six months. Each of the three systems has 1TB of storage (a total of 3TB), and each system will need an additional 2TB of storage each in the next twelve months. Therefore, the storage consolidation SAN requires 3TB of storage now plus 1.5TB for the first six months of growth. This configuration actually allows the hosts to grow exactly as if they had local storage. But storage now can be allocated to each host, as needed to accommodate uneven growth patterns.

This configuration requires the same amount of storage, but the timing of the deployment is different. The free pool of storage in the SAN can be equal to 1.5 times the size of a single host system's storage instead of 3 times the storage that a single host needs for growth. As a result, the storage consolidation SAN requires more frequent storage acquisitions to achieve the same growth rate, but allows the acquisitions to be smaller and the idle storage on the systems as a group to be smaller, because deployment is easier and more flexible.

PERFORMANCE REQUIREMENTS

An examination of the three ETL systems using the get_io.sh and get_iosize.pl scripts (Examples 3.1 and 3.2) sets the performance requirements for the ETL storage consolidation SAN. The bandwidth graphs in Figure 3.5 show widely varying usage from host system to host system.

Host 1 has the highest aggregate bandwidth and the least consistent usage timing even though the bandwidth utilization is mostly consistent. Hosts 2 and 3 have more consistent usage patterns and do not have extremely high bandwidth requirements. If it is decided to compromise on absolute bandwidth or if the peak workload on Host

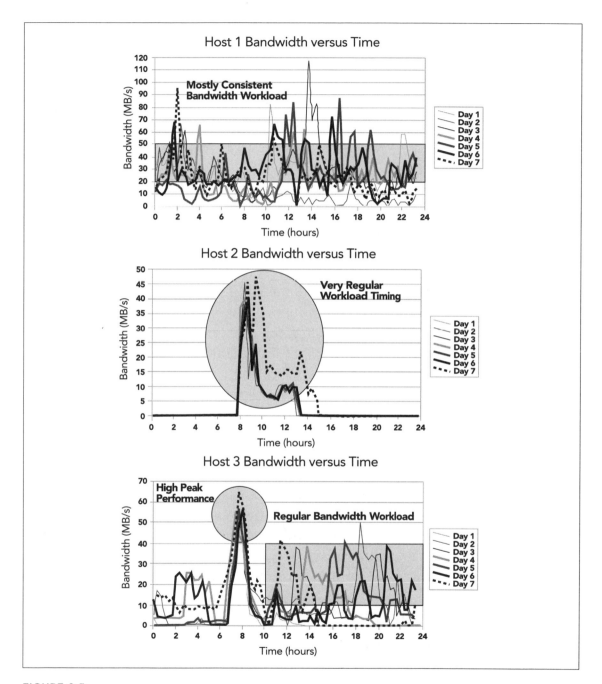

FIGURE 3.5

Three consolidation candidate host systems, bandwidth versus time

1 can be relocated to one of the other hosts during a less busy time, then the bandwidth requirement for this SAN can be set at 100MBps.

The IOPS requirements we see in Figure 3.6 show an average-to-high channel demand and an average overall demand for the combined requirements of these host systems.

This information, along with the preceding bandwidth information, enables us to select the following:

- The number of channels required per host system

- The number of channels per storage device

- The number of paths through the fabric per host system

The aggregate I/O size value for these host systems is not nearly as useful in this case due to the high number of overlapping jobs running on each host system. A full assessment of the characteristic I/O size for the systems requires a detailed application analysis of each job. It is not necessary to perform the assessment at this time because the other characteristics are much clearer, and they provide the necessary amount of information about the I/O behavior.

Analyzing I/O in Other SAN Types

Examining the I/O behaviors of a system for capacity planning or a new project is difficult because the system does not exist before the deployment of the SAN. These types of SANs do have some similarities to a storage consolidation SAN and can be assessed in the same way. The results of the assessment will have less certainty but still allow for the setting of SAN parameters that will hopefully achieve a good SAN design.

If a company deploys a new data warehouse application every three to six months, with the same amount of storage and layout, then it is useful to deploy a capacity-planning SAN using several of that application's host system types. Examine one of the prior data warehouse

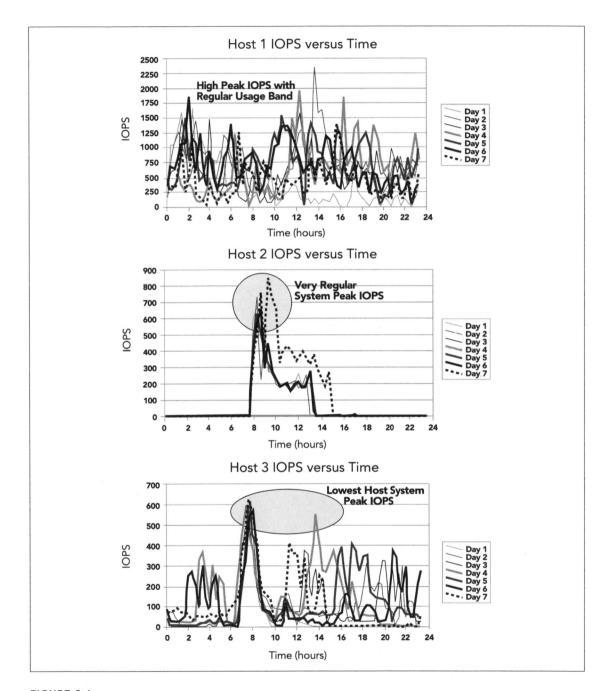

FIGURE 3.6

Three consolidation candidate host systems, IOPS versus time

host systems and then use it as a template for the host systems in the capacity-planning SAN. The advantage of this method, as opposed to just deploying some number of application host systems with directly attached storage, is that the capacity-planning SAN can accommodate changing requirements without any new physical work on the host systems or their storage.

If a new data warehouse application is expected to require twice the typical amount of storage that the template application host system has, the storage can easily be accommodated in the capacity-planning SAN by making changes to the SAN configuration that logically re-assigns storage. If deploying a group of host systems with directly attached storage where one host system needs an increase in storage size, the host must either have storage physically reconnected from some other host system or benefit from a new storage acquisition. This reconnection potentially leaves one host system short of disk space, takes longer than a configuration change, or requires an additional storage purchase, leaving other storage underutilized. The savings in labor alone will make this a worthwhile use of a SAN.

Use the same tools for examination of the template host system, but accept more variability in the design. The bandwidth assessment of a typical midsize data warehouse system in Figure 3.7 shows peak host bandwidth in the average range.

Take the per-channel I/O bandwidth into consideration when deciding the type of I/O channel to use and the required number per system. This choice can push the per-channel I/O bandwidth from the average range to the high range using four or fewer I/O channels per host system. Fewer than four low-bandwidth I/O channels can constrain peak bandwidth, but this design choice needs some justification because there is a potential for reduced performance.

The second graph in Figure 3.7 shows the IOPS behavior of the data warehouse template system. The system has a peak IOPS performance characteristic that is in the average region for a host, but the

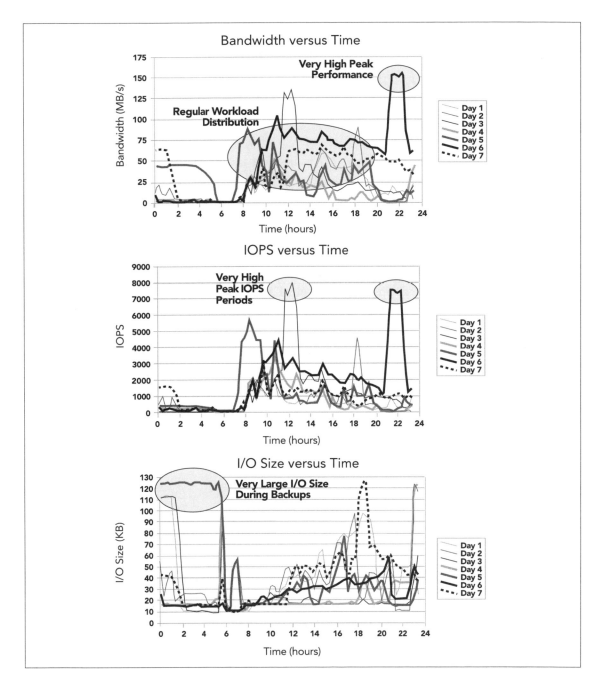

FIGURE 3.7

Data warehouse SAN candidate, host system I/O analysis

per-channel IOPS performance moves into the high performance region with fewer than six I/O channels available.

The system bandwidth and IOPS analysis shows that the peak bandwidth occurs at a different time than peak IOPS. A quick look at the I/O size during these times can rule out obvious errors in the IOPS or bandwidth assessments. In Figure 3.7, the I/O size during the peak bandwidth period is indeed larger than during the peak IOPS period. Another interesting characteristic to note is that the peak I/O size occurs during a low IOPS time but still requires a significant amount of bandwidth.

It is now possible to determine the number of I/O channels and the expected performance of the host systems on this capacity-planning SAN, based on the IOPS and bandwidth assessment. For example, one I/O channel should be allocated per host system for every 50MBps of bandwidth or every 1000 IOPS. Two I/O channels should be added for every 50MBps of bandwidth or 1000 IOPS if multipath I/O is required. The I/O size information helps validate the assessment and gives some useful information for creating an I/O model for design verification testing.

3.5 Simplified SAN Application I/O Models for Verification

Now that the performance assessment of the template applications and host systems has been completed, use the information gathered from the assessment to model the expected behaviors of the host systems. The verification model can be simple and should try to re-create the I/O behaviors of the system being modeled. Not all I/O behaviors need to be built into the model, because modeling everything is extremely complex and time-consuming. The verification model tries to emulate peak performance for the chosen I/O characteristics. The verification model can also test failure modes and evaluate SAN behaviors while working with specific features of the SAN.

Modeling the NAS Server Replacement

The I/O model for the NAS server replacement SAN in Figure 3.1 (page 59) should emulate the archival processes that the NAS server currently services. This application simultaneously transfers several large files to the NAS server, and the model for the file transfers can be quite simple. The tester places a set of test files on one client host system or more and then writes a simple set of scripts that transfers these files to and from the new SAN file server.

The tester then measures the transfers for bandwidth performance and checks for reliability. Performance should be evaluated and assessed from several places in the SAN. Ideally, the throughput of the NAS replacement SAN has been measured from the client, the server, and the fabric devices that make up the SAN.

Testing of the failure cases in the NAS replacement SAN includes these tasks:

- Simulating device failures during data transfers

- Powering off fabric devices

- Rebooting host systems

- Unplugging cables in a controlled manner to evaluate behaviors under failure or maintenance conditions

These tests provide a better understanding of the failure cases and may uncover problems in maintenance methods or the design.

Modeling the Data Warehouse ETL Consolidation SAN

A model for the storage consolidation SAN in Figure 3.4 (page 63) is more complex than the NAS replacement SAN test model. The systems in the storage consolidation SAN will use the fabric-attached storage for file creation in addition to reads and transfers, which differs from the dedicated data transfer use of the NAS replacement

SAN. The I/O model must include file creation, reads, and writes. Modeling must also include an approximation of the timing of the processes.

The first step is the creation of a few simple scripts that create, read, and write files. These scripts can then be grouped together to simulate I/O behaviors of the systems being consolidated on the SAN. Example 3.3 shows a Perl script that randomly reads a file.

This simple script performs a specified number of random 1KB reads throughout a specified file. A similar script in Perl can randomly write updates to a file, as shown in Example 3.4.

The writer.pl script inserts an all-zero, 1KB update into a specified file at a random location. It is easy to modify the size and content of the update for customization.

Much simpler scripts can also create files. Because a new file will be sequentially written with the typical I/O size of the application in most cases, a file creation script can use the UNIX system tool *dd*. Example 3.5 shows a *dd* command to write an 800MB file in 8KB-size blocks.

In Example 3.5, the parameters are:

- Input file (if)

- Output file (of)

- Block size (bs)

- Number of IOPS (count)

To create a file of any size with any I/O size, change the block size and the count.

Use a wrapper script to run the scripts or file creation command numerous times. Simulate CPU processing time with delays in the wrapper. A wrapper script that simulates a load operation in a data warehouse is shown in Example 3.6.

EXAMPLE 3.3.   A random file reader script (reader.pl)

```perl
#!/usr/local/bin/perl
#
# reader.pl
# Perform random reads of a file
#

# The first argument to the script is the file name
# The second argument to the script is the number
# of reads to perform
$file = $ARGV[0];
$count = $ARGV[1];

# open the file to be read and find its size
open(FH, $file) || die "Can't open $file\n";
seek(FH, 0, 2);
$filesize = tell(FH);
close(FH);

srand(time);

open(FH, $file) || die "Can't open $file\n";

# perform 1KB reads of the file at random offsets
# $count times
while ( $i <= $count) {
    $fpos = int(rand $filesize) + 1;
    read(FH, $dump, 1024);
    $i++;
    }

close(FH);
printf "Done reading file $file\n";
```

EXAMPLE 3.4.   A random file updater script (writer.pl)

```perl
#!/usr/local/bin/perl
# writer.pl
# Perform random updates of a file
#
$LOCK_SH = 1;
$LOCK_EX = 2;
$LOCK_NB = 4;
$LOCK_UN = 8;
# The first argument to the script is the file name
# The second argument to the script is the number of writes to perform
$file = $ARGV[0];
$count = $ARGV[1];

# Make a 1KB buffer of zeros
$buf="0" x 1024;

# open the file to be read and find its size
open(FH, $file) || die "Can't open $file\n";
seek(FH, 0, 2);
$filesize = tell(FH);
close(FH);

srand(time);

# open and lock the file for writing
open(FH, "+<$file") || die "Can't open $file\n";
flock(FH, $LOCK_EX);

# perform 1KB writes to the file at random offsets $count times
while ( $i <= $count) {
    $fpos = int(rand $filesize) - 1;
    seek(FH, $fpos, 0);
    print FH $buf;
    $i++;
    }

flock(FH, $LOCK_UN);
close(FH);
```

EXAMPLE 3.5. Simple file creation using *dd*

```
dd if=/dev/zero of=/fs1/file01 bs=8192 count=100000
```

EXAMPLE 3.6. Data warehouse load simulation wrapper

```
#!/bin/sh
# Data warehouse load I/O model

# create 10 2GB files sequentially
dd if=/dev/zero of=/fs1/file01 bs=8192 count=250000
dd if=/dev/zero of=/fs1/file02 bs=8192 count=250000
dd if=/dev/zero of=/fs1/file03 bs=8192 count=250000
dd if=/dev/zero of=/fs1/file04 bs=8192 count=250000
dd if=/dev/zero of=/fs1/file05 bs=8192 count=250000
dd if=/dev/zero of=/fs1/file06 bs=8192 count=250000
dd if=/dev/zero of=/fs1/file07 bs=8192 count=250000
dd if=/dev/zero of=/fs1/file08 bs=8192 count=250000
dd if=/dev/zero of=/fs1/file09 bs=8192 count=250000
dd if=/dev/zero of=/fs1/file10 bs=8192 count=250000

# read and write previously created
# simulated catalog file at random
# 250000 times simultaneously in
# 10000 I/O chunks with 30 seconds
# of simulated calculations between chunks
i=1
while [ $i -le 25 ]
do
  reader.pl /fs1/simucat 10000 &
  writer.pl /fs1/simucat 10000 &
  i=`expr $i + 1`
  sleep 30
done
```

These tools simulate the I/O workload of the ETL systems on the storage consolidation SAN. Use the same I/O workload simulation for failure mode and maintenance evaluation by simulating failures and performing maintenance tasks while the model runs.

Model the I/O behaviors of the systems on a capacity-planning SAN for midsize data warehouse applications using the same set of tools. In addition, use a nonrandom read command, because data warehouse systems tend to scan large tables sequentially. Example 3.7 shows a *dd* command that performs a simple sequential read.

This command reads 8KB blocks of the file created in Example 3.5. In this case the command simply reads and discards the data because the data is not needed for anything else.

The four simple I/O workload components just described can be assembled to simulate the I/O behavior of the data warehouse systems in almost any mode. Simulation of the staging, loading, and querying of the data warehouse system requires several wrapper scripts in order to combine these I/O workload driver tools. The wrapper scripts would be variations on Example 3.6 and can also be very simple.

In a capacity-planning SAN where zone changes can be frequent due to unknown initial system configurations, evaluation of zoning changes is particularly interesting. Make changes to the capacity-planning SAN configuration while running the I/O model to determine the exact behavior of the systems, fabric devices, and storage devices.

Create an experimental SAN I/O model out of the same components used for the capacity-planning SAN in order to exploit the SAN performance characteristic or behavior. Running several copies of the sequential reader at the same time will drive up bandwidth on the SAN. Multiple copies of the random reader and writer scripts will create high IOPS loads. Additional combinations of the I/O work-

EXAMPLE 3.7.   Simple sequential read using *dd*

```
dd if=/fs1/file01 of=/dev/null bs=8192 count=100000
```

load components can simulate the interesting workloads found in most environments.

Model a SAN for a new project in the same fashion as an experimental SAN. The SAN for a new project has more clearly defined performance expectations that facilitate a more accurate model of the expected I/O workload. The SAN does not have to be intentionally stressed, but it can be evaluated with an I/O model that creates the expected performance level for the host systems and applications that will be using the SAN.

3.6 Final Project Definition

Use the information from assessments of the system and application I/O characteristics to define the project parameters. The type of SAN and the I/O behaviors point to the performance parameters and host system behavior expectations. The project definition also takes into account failure modes and other operational considerations such as dynamic SAN reconfiguration. Use the definition as a yardstick for measuring whether or not the goals of the SAN have been accomplished.

NAS Replacement SAN Definition

The definition of the design for the NAS replacement SAN is fairly simple. (See Figure 3.1 on page 59.) The parameters that drive the design are the bandwidth required for the application and multipath I/O channel infrastructure that prevents a systems outage in the case of a single I/O channel failure.

The bandwidth required is minimal, with a peak measured usage of 13MBps. This means that any single Ultra SCSI or Fibre Channel I/O interface can meet the bandwidth requirement for this SAN. The multipath I/O channel configuration requires a minimum of two channels per host system or storage system. Because two I/O channels provide from 72MBps to 200MBps, depending on the selected type, the bandwidth requirement can easily be met. The SAN requires 1TB of storage to accommodate its current data set and an additional 0.5TB of storage to accommodate six months of growth. All of the interconnections between fabric devices, if any are necessary, will also require two I/O channels.

Storage Consolidation SAN Definition

The definition of the storage consolidation SAN project is more complicated due to higher performance requirements and more trade-offs to accommodate the different host systems and applications. (See Figure 3.4 on page 63.) Fabric bandwidth is one of the defining parameters of the SAN. Although only one of the systems has bandwidth requirements in even the average range for a single host system, the bandwidth requirements of all the systems being consolidated must be serviced concurrently on the SAN fabric. The storage consolidation SAN requires a multipath I/O channel configuration for failure resilience and load balancing, if possible. This SAN supports a data warehouse ETL workload, so the SAN includes a data movement tool that improves data transfer times and removes load from the consolidated host system's IP networks.

Aggregate bandwidths of 400MBps in the fabric and 100MBps per host system are necessary in this SAN. This performance should be adequate given a more evenly balanced workload across all of the systems. A balanced workload eliminates the spikes in the peak usage of the one host system with needs that exceed 100MBps. The SAN requires at least a pair of Ultra SCSI II controllers (or faster) to meet the SAN host system performance requirements. Because of the multiple controllers required for bandwidth, the multiple channel I/O failover and load balancing configuration requirement can also be met. The storage space required for this SAN is 4.5TB at the start.

This allocation provides storage space for the current data set on all three host systems, plus the capability to grow all three host systems by 0.5TB or any individual host system by up to 1.5TB on an immediate need basis.

Capacity-Planning SAN Definition

The bandwidth and flexibility requirements of the host systems characterize the project definition for the data warehouse capacity-planning SAN. The requirements also include a multiple I/O channel configuration for host system and storage device resilience. Features include data replication for scalability and disaster recovery that support the business-critical data warehouses targeted for the SAN.

Each host system requires 200MBps of bandwidth for storage devices, and the fabric must support the aggregate traffic of four host systems. These requirements mean that the fabric will require 800MBps of bandwidth to support the concurrent load of the host systems. The storage devices must also support the 200MBps from each host system either individually or as a group, depending on their size and the final allocation to each system. Two Fibre Channel I/O channels can meet the bandwidth and multiple I/O channel failover needs of each system. Only two I/O channels require high per-channel IOPS performance, so a trade-off that installs more I/O controllers to meet the IOPS needs of the host systems may be necessary. A higher number of the same, or lower, performance I/O channels can meet the IOPS needs of the host systems and provide a lower per-channel IOPS solution. However, the lower performance I/O channels might not meet the bandwidth needs.

The storage space requirement for the capacity-planning SAN is 1TB per deployed system or 4TB total to start. It is likely that there will be data growth, so some expansion capacity can be built into the SAN. To provide for the data replication scheme, the SAN requires installation of some additional fabric connectivity in order to increase available bandwidth without slowing the data warehouse application systems usage. Chapter 4 shows how the host design parameters defined here can translate into useful SAN designs.

Other SAN Types

The SAN design definition for a new project is set to meet the requirements of the project. A good strategy for setting these requirements involves finding applications or host systems that may have performance and host system needs that meet the requirements of the new project. Then apply the parameters of those systems to the new project SAN.

The design for an experimental SAN meets the testing requirements of the SAN. For example, if performing IOPS-limit evaluations, then use a low number of channels and a high IOPS–capable storage device. If testing failover under stress, then specify at least one alternate I/O channel. Test SAN limits and behaviors by constraining the I/O parameter to be tested and then observing what happens to the host systems, storage devices, and fabric devices when an extreme load is placed on the SAN.

3.7 Summary

Using the tools described in this chapter, I/O analysis can be completed and the SAN project type can be determined. All planning aspects of the SAN project should now be finalized. Next, the design stage can begin: time to select the components, create I/O models for validation, plan the physical integration, and start evaluating trade-offs.

4

SAN DESIGN

The design phase of a SAN project applies the information gathered during the investigation of application and host system I/O behaviors in order to formulate a working SAN. Design decisions include the selection of hardware, software, and connectivity. Comparing I/O requirements to component features narrows the number of choices. The final SAN design must meet all of the requirements defined in the project analysis. Physical implementation must also be possible.

The specification of SAN components is the last part of the design process before SAN assembly and deployment. The selection of components comes from hardware devices and software capable of servicing the SAN design requirements. It is helpful to select components familiar to the implementers in order to simplify the deployment of those components through familiar management and configuration methods.

4.1 Hardware Components

SAN hardware components consist of host systems, HBAs, fabric devices, storage devices, and special-purpose SAN devices.

Host Systems and HBAs

Host systems and HBAs are selected together to eliminate compatibility problems. The desired host system type generally narrows the available HBA choices, and the specific HBA features desired then further narrow the choices. If more than one option remains, the specific environment determines the final HBA selection.

Common choices for host systems and HBAs are Sun Microsystems UNIX systems with SBus I/O channels and JNI Corporation's HBAs for SBus. The SBus I/O channel in the host system requires an SBus-based HBA. There are several possible HBA vendor choices when using SBus-based host systems, but the HBA must be compatible with the host system I/O bus. For PCI-based host systems, there are more HBA options from different vendors than for SBus-based systems. Other host system I/O architectures require HBAs specific to those architectures.

Storage and Fabric Devices

Storage devices that meet the performance and storage feature requirements of the SAN are widely available for most possible design parameters. Selection factors include:

- Compatibility of storage and fabric devices

- Connectivity and flexibility provided by specific fabric devices

Use vendor-specific assessment to research this information.

Incompatibilities can cause unnecessary problems. Unintelligent disk enclosures or Just-a-Bunch-of-Disks (JBOD) storage devices are examples of devices that can have compatibility problems in fabric environments. JBODs generally have to be isolated from the rest of the fabric-aware devices in some way, making them less flexible. A single JBOD device or disk enclosure cannot be split between host systems, creating the potential for unused space that cannot be redeployed. This limitation has an adverse effect on storage consolidation SANs, if not other SAN types.

Fabric devices make up the SAN I/O interconnections. These devices include:

- Bridges that connect non-native fabric devices

- Hubs that increase connectivity while maintaining the performance level of a single I/O channel

- Switches that increase connectivity and improve performance

Switches and hubs are selected to provide connectivity and flexibility in the SAN. Switches provide most of the infrastructure in a SAN; they can increase connectivity in the same way as hubs, but they can also raise available performance. The performance increase provided by switches comes from the multiple point-to-point connections possible in a switch, instead of just repeating traffic on all ports as hubs do. Switch selection can also take advantage of features that complement storage devices and host systems.

SAN fabric switch devices currently do not interoperate across vendors and may not for some time to come. There was a great deal of work done in 2001, and some vendors, but not many, have stated that they have true switch interoperability now or will sometime in 2002. As time goes on, this switch interoperability will be an available option, making SAN fabric switch device selection easier through support for more than one switch device type in the same SAN fabric. Bridges and hubs do not have interoperability problems because they are mostly passive devices.

Fabric device solutions include Fibre Channel switches from numerous vendors such as Brocade Communications Systems, Gadzoox Networks, McDATA Corporation, QLogic Corporation, and Vixel Corporation. Fibre Channel hubs are also available from a wide variety of vendors. Storage devices used in a SAN need to be capable of running properly in a fabric environment. Intelligent storage devices from vendors like EMC Corporation, Hewlett-Packard, Hitachi Data Systems, and others are capable of running in a fabric environment without problems. The manufacturers, SAN integrators, or both verify that all of these devices work properly in a SAN environment. Many JBOD storage devices can also function in a SAN environment.

Special-Purpose Devices

Special-purpose SAN devices are beginning to appear in order to support resource allocation and service functions that are external to all other SAN hardware components. Special-purpose devices usually handle a single service, such as metadata control for file sharing. As these devices become more sophisticated, they can begin to provide more functionality in a single device. Factors in the selection of a special-purpose device include:

- Features supported by the device

- Compatibility with the SAN hardware

Compatibility is critical for special-purpose devices because they have a very limited set of supported devices, making them useless with other devices. Examples of common special-purpose devices include virtualization systems like the SN6000 from StorageTek and the RamSan solid-state storage devices from Texas Memory Systems.

4.2 Software Components

Software components for use in a SAN consist of the following:

- Host operating systems

- HBA device drivers

- Fabric device operating firmware

- Storage device operating firmware

- SAN service software

- Storage service software

For compatibility reasons, hardware selection controls the selection of most software components.

Host Operating Systems

The host systems selection determines the choice of the host operating system. However, more than one operating system can be available for a hardware platform. Factors in the choice of a host operating system include:

- The application planned for the host system

- The level of SAN support available in the host operating system

- The flexibility of device configuration in the host operating system

Choose the host operating system with the best SAN support, if at all possible. An evaluation of device addressing and configuration with respect to the target environment is important. It is best to use host operating systems that have good support for SANs and have an understandable method for addressing SAN devices. If SAN devices are presented in a logical and coherent way, then the configuration of the SAN devices is simplified. Individual devices can be identified easily and configurations can be constructed to place data in the best location for the I/O behaviors required. Almost all host operating systems available can be used in SANs today.

HBA Device Drivers

The host operating system and the HBA itself determine HBA device driver selection. Multiple HBAs may be used with the same host system type, so the hardware and HBA driver must be selected to match the host system hardware and the host operating system. The HBA driver selected should also be evaluated for configurability and features that may make the driver more appropriate to the specific SAN. HBA driver configuration options may include one or more of the following:

- Loop attach mode

- Fabric attach mode

- IP over Fibre Channel mode

- HBA-specific options

HBAs with a loop attach mode run the arbitrated loop Fibre Channel protocol. HBAs with a fabric attach mode are able to log in to a Fibre Channel network for communications. IP over Fibre Channel support in an HBA provides an IP network protocol stack that runs over the Fibre Channel link established by the HBA. Devices from Troika Networks include multipath awareness in the driver, which is an example of a SAN-specific driver feature.

Fabric Device Firmware

Fabric device operating firmware is selected with respect to a specific firmware version as opposed to different firmware types, because only one firmware is available for each device from each vendor. The version of the firmware is selected with a balance of stability and features in mind. A newer firmware version may take advantage of specific feature enhancements, even if reliability is less well known. Firmware version selection should also take into account expected switch stability as well as all vendor qualifications of hardware and software. A reliance on complete qualification is not necessary, because many firmware versions that have not been qualified can work. The firmware qualification process is different for each vendor of SAN devices, even though in many cases multiple vendors provide the same exact device under different OEM agreements. SAN vendors are actively working to establish industry-wide software and hardware qualification and standardization[1] in order to make SAN component selection simpler.

Examples of fabric device firmware features include zoning, SNMP management, and Quality of Service (QoS). Zoning in fabric devices is usually implemented on a port or WWN basis for fabric traffic isolation. SNMP management in the fabric firmware allows standard network management tools to manage the SAN fabric devices. Firmware that has a basic way to differentiate high- and low-priority data traffic types can perform crude SAN QoS management.

Storage Device Firmware

In almost all cases, storage vendors choose the operating firmware at delivery time, and the current version of storage firmware is usually the only one available. Vendors actively encourage users to upgrade to the latest mature firmware version in order to reduce the risk of known bugs. However, storage firmware may also add features, so there is always a chance that new bugs can occur when using new storage device firmware. Selecting the right firmware for storage devices is usually a matter of getting a sufficiently stable and supported version. This selection sometimes involves a trade-off between desired features and risk. Older firmware versions tend to be more stable, since the bugs have been found and fixed, but new features can be required for the application using the storage. The most mature version of firmware with the desired features is usually the version that will be selected, but a more risk-inclined implementation may use firmware with more advanced features in favor of stability.

Some examples of storage device firmware features include RAID data protection, remote block data copy, and snapshot data copy. Several RAID data-protection schemes are implemented in storage devices to provide different combinations of relative risk and overall

---

1. See http://www.snia.org/English/Committees/Interoperability/index.html for details about interoperability and testing standards.

performance of the storage system. Remote block data copy for disaster recovery creates an additional copy of critical data at a geographically distant site from the source of the data. Snapshot data copy creates additional copies of a data set for any number of uses, including backups, quality assurance testing, and data access scalability.

SAN Service Software

SAN service software offers tools that implement a target service, such as LUN masking. Most SAN service software is specific to the host system or the storage device. Software for implementing SAN services may also be completely independent of the devices and work at the application level. Common SAN services include LUN masking and data sharing.

The desired functionality and the manageability of the software tools should guide your choice of the SAN services software. For example, software integrated into an existing system in the SAN is much easier to deploy. Deployment is simpler because the hosting device needs to be configured only for the software and requires no additional devices.

Storage Service Software

Storage service software implements both SAN features and storage device features. Storage device vendors, SAN device vendors, and third-party vendors offer extensive software choices. The exact software choices depend on the storage services to be implemented. Storage services include:

- Data replication
- Data transfer
- File sharing
- Data snapshot

Storage services such as data replication and snapshot copies of data can be implemented in a number of ways. If storage devices are all from the same vendor, then a data snapshot tool from that storage device vendor is a good choice. If the storage devices are from multiple vendors, then a third-party application is needed to implement data snapshots across the storage devices. Storage service software includes the following:

- ControlCenter, from EMC Corporation, for storage allocation and control of data copy features in storage devices from EMC

- SANPoint Control, from VERITAS Software Corporation, which provides multi-vendor support for storage allocation and monitoring

- SANsymphony, from DataCore Software Corporation, which offers allocation and resource pooling for multi-vendor storage virtualization

4.3 SAN Component Map

Figure 4.1 shows a map that depicts the process of selecting SAN components. The map can be redrawn for any SAN project using the components that may be selected for use. In order to create the map, the available components should be grouped by type and then matched with devices in the other groups for stated or tested compatibility. The connections from component to component indicate that they can be used together. The map provides a basis for tracing multiple paths end to end from an application to the storage devices. The resulting paths determine a list of components to choose from when building a SAN for a particular application.

For example, Application 1 can use Host type 1, HBA type 1, HBA type 2, or HBA type 3; Switch type 1 or Switch type 2; Storage device type 1, Storage device type 2, or Storage device type 3. While it appears that there are still many devices to choose from, 25 percent

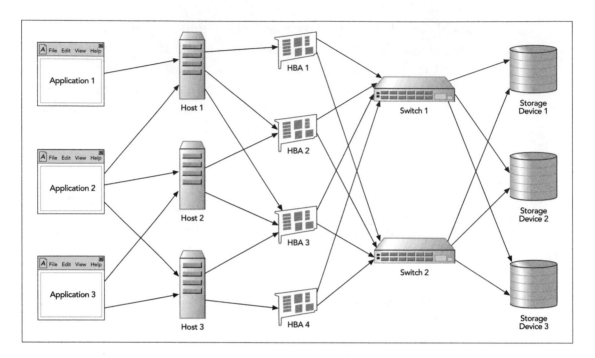

FIGURE 4.1

SAN component selection map

have been eliminated by simple incompatibilities—a fairly good start for component selection. Three of the twelve possible components have been eliminated easily, without the need for evaluation. Application 1 cannot use Host type 2 or Host type 3, so HBA type 4 can also be discarded. These components account for three of the possible twelve being considered, leaving 75 percent of the original components to choose from. The map shows the application-to-storage selection path, but almost any component in the SAN can be a starting point for the same type of process.

4.4 Component Selection by SAN Type

The component selections in this section are specific to the SAN types first described in Chapter 1.

NAS Replacement SAN

For the NAS replacement SAN, the selected hardware components need to accommodate the SAN file-sharing software server. Additional selection criteria include client and storage system connectivity options. The host system choices are based on the existing NAS configuration. In turn, the host systems determine HBA choices because HBAs selected for the connectivity of the host systems are specific to the host system's I/O buses. The selection of HBAs is limited to one type of HBA per host system type, in order to reduce the number of possible configurations. The host system vendor, if possible, should provide the HBA selected for each host system type in order to achieve the best configuration stability and support for the device. The next best HBA selection comes from a vendor who meets your requirements. Many HBAs are OEM parts from the same manufacturer, making HBA familiarity more common than the available choices seem to indicate.

Storage devices for the NAS replacement SAN need to provide simply the space for storage and the capability to present the storage to multiple host systems at the fabric level. The sharing application takes care of the data movement, storage, and retrieval on the host systems. A RAM cache in the storage device may be useful to improve metadata update performance. To accommodate the 1.5TB of required storage, the designer selects a pair of 1TB storage devices with 4GB RAM caches. This is 0.5TB more space than specified, but the deployment of the second complete 1TB unit simplifies the implementation by preventing the reconfiguration of the storage device when demand exceeds 0.5TB. The 4GB RAM caches in these storage devices are the typical minimum sizes for large, enterprise-class storage devices. The combined cache is only 0.4 percent of the total available storage; the cache is not really large and can be effective only for the most reused data, such as the data-sharing metadata.

The only fabric devices selected for the NAS replacement SAN are Fibre Channel switches. There is no need for port fanout with hubs in this SAN, because there is sufficient connectivity. Media conversion with SCSI-to-Fibre-Channel bridges is also unnecessary. The total number of systems and storage devices on the SAN can determine the total number of SAN fabric devices. The number of fabric devices depends on the number of ports per fabric device when compared to the total number of systems and storage devices with two connections. If using more than one fabric device, fabric device interconnection requires a certain number of overhead ports.

Using a configuration consisting of a sixteen-port fabric device with ten host systems and storage devices requires two fabric devices to provide two channels for each device connected to the SAN. This configuration provides a total of thirty-two ports with twenty initially in use. The fabric devices then provide multiple paths from the host systems to the storage.

The best way to configure this SAN physically is to run redundant connections to each fabric device from each host system and storage device with a single InterSwitch Link (ISL) for management purposes. Switch-to-switch connections are referred to as ISLs to denote an internal fabric connection as opposed to a device-to-fabric connection. The management ISL is not necessary for the functionality of the SAN, but it simplifies management tasks by allowing the pair of switches to function as a single fabric. A larger configuration with four switches can be used to provide a configuration with two tiers and multiple ISLs: one tier provides storage device attachment; the other tier is used for host device attachment. This configuration has the advantage of greater expansion capability, but it is also more complex. See Figure 4.4 (on page 102) for an example of a tiered SAN topology.

Selection of software for the NAS replacement SAN begins with the choice of the SAN-based data-sharing software. This choice influences the selection of other software and hardware components. For example, the host systems supported by the sharing software server point to the choices for the hardware components of the data-sharing server host system. In addition, the client host systems supported by the data-sharing software determine which client host system types can be used on this SAN.

You must choose the supported host operating systems for the client and server components of the file-sharing software with respect to the host systems using the SAN. Avoid incompatibilities or unsupported host system operating system versions in order to prevent usability and stability problems.

Storage Consolidation SAN

The components for the storage consolidation SAN need to provide flexible connectivity to storage as well as a path for the SAN data movement tool. This approach reduces complexity because the SAN provides connectivity only. The data movement feature software selected for the consolidation SAN does not require additional devices.

Choose the HBAs for the host systems migrated to this SAN to enable connectivity for the host systems only. Any existing storage device connectivity must be replaced or used with a bridge device, if necessary, unless the storage device is already a Fibre Channel device.

Storage devices selected for the storage consolidation SAN need to accommodate the 4.5TB of data being migrated from the existing host system's direct-access storage and the specified 1.5TB storage space for growth. A selection of 1TB storage devices meets the storage requirements of the SAN as well and provides the required connectivity and features.

The implementation of the data movement application also uses a feature of the storage devices. Therefore, all host systems require connectivity to the storage devices that implement the data movement application. Caches in the storage devices may be ineffective due to the mixed workload of the host systems, leading to configuration at minimum size. The extensive data transfer and large file processing typical of ETL systems may not see an advantage from large storage device caches. Use of small caches in the storage devices improves access to the most reused data.

The fabric devices must be switches in order to avoid potential bandwidth problems. In a storage consolidation SAN, the performance requirements are somewhat high. Port fanout with hubs is difficult to implement without creating a potential bandwidth shortfall. The switches must be sized for measured bandwidth, the required total number of ports, and manageability. Two sixteen-port fabric devices are the minimum to support the three host systems and six storage devices with the required multiple connections. However, these numbers create an awkward configuration.

A better configuration uses storage device and host system tiers, because this configuration should be the most expandable. This configuration requires four fabric devices. Fabric devices with higher port counts are more efficient, but not all vendors have switches with more than sixteen ports. When available, devices with higher port counts can be used to collapse SAN fabrics based on groups of smaller switches, if desired. This configuration uses redundant host system connections to one pair of switches and redundant storage device connections to the other pair of switches. All four of these switches then connect to two other switches with redundant ISLs.

The storage consolidation SAN has simpler software selection requirements because this SAN does not use application-level features. The storage consolidation SAN therefore requires only the selection of compatible host operating systems together with management tools. The compatibility of the host operating systems needs only to be sufficient to ensure that there is no interference with the operation of foreign host systems, because none of the host systems on the storage consolidation SAN shares anything but the fabric, for connectivity.

Capacity-Planning SAN

For a capacity-planning SAN, select hardware components based on the most common host systems used for data warehouse applications. The capacity-planning SAN provides a ready-to-use set of host systems and storage devices with a generic configuration for hosting data warehousing applications. The host systems provide a set level of performance with a variable storage capacity, and a drastically shortened deployment time, because the SAN is already assembled. The capacity-planning SAN also provides a data replication mechanism as a feature.

The capacity-planning SAN includes two different host system types, chosen to coexist on the same SAN without problems. They provide a more flexible configuration for deployment of the possible data warehouse types. The two system types can potentially use the same HBA with different drivers for each host system. These simplifications improve host system compatibility in the SAN and allow easier connection of the different host systems.

HBA selection criteria include:

- Compatibility

- Configurability

- Flexibility

The HBA configuration flexibility is particularly important because the capacity-planning SAN must accommodate several different potential uses.

The devices are 1TB intelligent storage devices that include a built-in block data replication mechanism. Each storage device has four

Fibre Channel connections to the SAN fabric. The SAN requires installation of four storage devices to meet the 4TB initial space requirement.

This SAN uses a tiered topology (described in Section 4.5) for host systems and storage device connectivity. A configuration of sixteen port switches with redundant paths and enough ISLs for the bandwidth requires four switches: two switches reside in the host system tier, and two switches reside in the storage tier. The four hosts and four storage devices with redundant connections to separate switches require a total of thirty-two switch ports. The ISLs for the SAN require sixteen additional ports. The forty-eight total ports required for this fabric leaves sixteen ports for additional connectivity or additional capacity. Any expansion can easily be accommodated with the excess ports in the SAN.

The software component selection process for the capacity-planning SAN resembles the process for the storage consolidation SAN. The host systems on the capacity-planning SAN are unlikely to share anything other than physical interconnections, so the host systems require only basic compatibility.

Storage device software component selection is more complicated because the expected use of the systems is not known in advance. Selection of as many storage device software components as possible facilitates flexibility of storage devices at deployment. Snapshot copy, data replication, and data transfer features of the storage devices are useful and should be selected if supported.

New Project SAN

The hardware selection for a new project SAN closely ties to the software application being hosted. The host systems must run the application as effectively as possible. The new project SAN allows host systems of the same type to run the same application or complementary applications while taking advantage of the SAN features and common connectivity. The number of host systems depends on the required performance and the SAN features chosen.

The HBAs are all identical because the host systems are all identical. Selection of the HBAs supports host systems connectivity as well as any SAN features selected for the new project applications.

The I/O performance and I/O behaviors required by the host systems running the new application determine selection of the storage devices. The amount of storage required by the new application also helps to identify the storage device, based on the expected data size and a certain amount of overhead for short-term growth and sizing inaccuracies. The overhead should be somewhere between 25 and 100 percent, depending on the expected growth in one acquisition cycle and the sizing estimate confidence. The overhead space is easier to estimate and smaller as more projects are deployed on SANs and measurement methods improve.

Fabric devices need to allow for a flexible configuration with excess performance at deployment. This flexibility and performance overhead enables the SAN to be adjusted in the case of sizing inaccuracies. A two-tiered configuration is also effective for deployment in a new project SAN, allowing for independent expansion of either storage or host system resources.

The selection of software components depends on the expected application needs of the new project. The first step is selection of any specific SAN feature software required by the new project. Then choose the server host system operating system that supports the SAN feature software. The last step is the selection of the host system operating system software that is required by the new project application from the supported client platforms of the SAN feature software.

Experimental SAN

In an experimental SAN, the number of devices is usually low. This limited number of devices enables more focused investigations. The small device count is helpful unless the goal is an investigation of scalability, which requires large numbers. One or two host systems are sufficient to investigate most SAN behaviors in an experimental SAN.

The HBAs used in an experimental SAN support simple connectivity or some SAN feature. For example, HBAs in an experimental SAN can be selected with a high capacity for the I/O parameter being stressed in testing:

- High IOPS performance HBAs for high IOPS investigations

- High throughput HBAs to investigate bandwidth behaviors of the SAN

HBAs with other features may also be selected for special purposes. Many HBAs are available with a wide variety of performance characteristics, so selection will have to be specific to the I/O behavior under examination.

The storage devices need to be capable of providing a flexible amount of storage and performance for SAN experiments. An intelligent storage device is the best choice, because it can be reconfigured logically and it should be capable of servicing a wide variety of I/O behaviors.

Base selection of SAN fabric devices is focused on configuration flexibility and high numbers of features. A device with extensive features enables more experiments without hardware replacement. A reduction in the effort required to reconfigure the fabric devices can also help when performing multiple experiments on the SAN.

The selection of experimental SAN software components depends on the SAN aspect under investigation. If the only area of interest is hardware performance, then no software components other than those for basic server, storage, and fabric compatibility are necessary. The selection of specific SAN feature software drives the selection of the other SAN software components, as in all the other SAN types.

4.5 SAN Topologies

The topology of the fabric device interconnections needs to be carefully considered in order to provide the required performance and availability. A simple and logical physical layout of the devices is also important for failure detection and resolution. The logical and physical attributes of devices that make up a SAN should also correlate to each other as effectively as possible. (See Chapter 5 for information on implementation.)

Simple Topologies

There are several useful topologies for physical SAN layout. For small SANs, star and flat topologies are adequate. These topologies are difficult to scale for large SANs.

In a star topology, the center of the star becomes the switch device, and the host systems and storage devices become the points. For example, in Figure 4.2, a Fibre Channel switch is the center of the star, and the six hosts and four storage devices are the points. The star is a useful configuration if the number of required device connections does not exceed the capacity of the central device. The use of hubs creates more connectivity, but the absolute performance of the SAN remains constant.

A flat topology SAN connects multiple star topologies, but some of the star points are other fabric devices instead of host systems. For example, switches or hubs can be connected to the SAN to add additional connectivity for host systems or storage devices. In Figure 4.3, a pair of Fibre Channel switches is connected to form a flat SAN

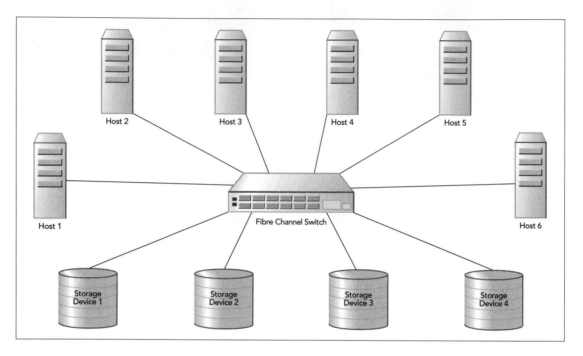

FIGURE 4.2

Star SAN topology

topology, with more connectivity than a star topology that uses a single Fibre Channel switch. This configuration allows more devices to be connected to the SAN.

The flat topology simplifies physical layout but can create problems for growth and performance. A star topology SAN that grows in an unplanned way usually transforms into a flat topology SAN, which is a convenient way to grow a SAN that has increasing connectivity requirements. The availability of the systems using a flat SAN topology can be a problem, because more fabric devices need to be traversed for a host system to connect to storage devices. Every device in a flat topology SAN has the potential to become a possible point of failure.

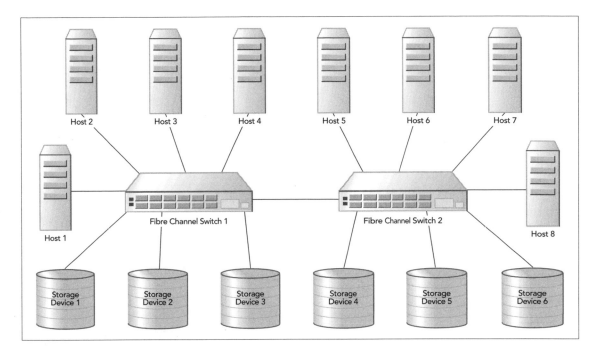

FIGURE 4.3

Flat SAN topology

Complex Topologies

For larger SANs, three topologies are more efficient:

- Full mesh

- Two-tier

- Backbone-core and edge

Each accommodates growth while providing a consistent performance level and improving fault isolation. These are complex topologies that require planning for the logical configuration and the physical layout. The physical layout of a large SAN should create a consistent set of standards for the logical configuration to follow, such as the specific physical ports on all switches to be used for ISLs, host connections, or storage connections.

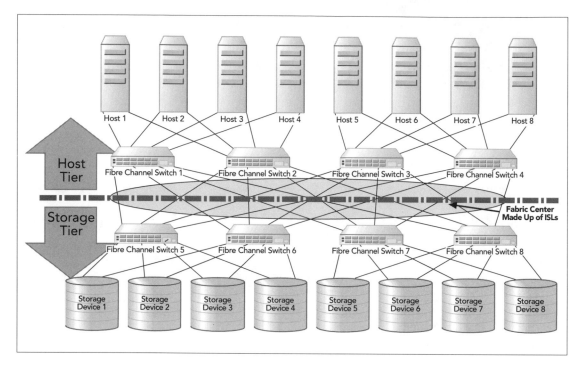

FIGURE 4.4

Tiered SAN topology

In Figure 4.4, a redundant two-tier layout has two sets of switches connected through a number of ISLs that provide the required redundancy and performance in the fabric. One set of switches connects only to storage devices, and the other set of switches connects only to host systems. This isolation of devices enables a more segmented configuration of the SAN. Segmentation enables better logical configurations and improved isolation of the relationships between storage devices and host systems. Host systems and storage devices are then connected to the fabric through multiple switches but only one of the tiers. These connections are usually made to two or more redundant switch devices, depending on the performance requirements of the SAN.

A full mesh topology requires the connection of all fabric devices to all other fabric devices, as shown in Figure 4.5. This topology

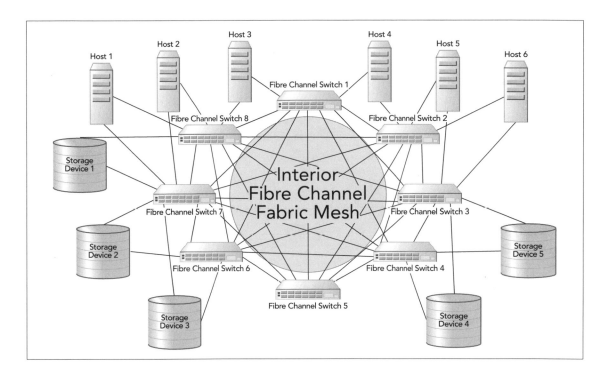

FIGURE 4.5

Full mesh SAN topology

requires more ISLs than a tiered topology, but it is useful if the links between switches are unreliable or if all devices on the SAN need to exchange data. A full mesh provides the same connectivity at any connection point but requires more overhead, while reducing isolation when implementing the logical configuration on top of the physical configuration. The full mesh topology is extremely useful for a SAN that connects multiple, geographically separate sites. In this case, a site can still be reached from at least one other link, even if a link is broken.

The backbone-and-edge topology makes use of multiple switch devices with different port counts or performance capacities. Redundantly connected larger switches with more ports and higher performance capacities form a high-speed core for data traffic, as shown in Figure 4.6. This topology uses smaller switches with fewer

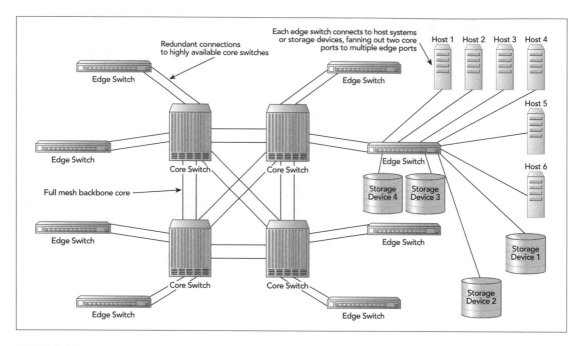

FIGURE 4.6

Backbone-and-edge SAN topology

ports and lower performance capabilities to fan out connections from the core switches to the host systems and storage devices. The number of edge ports dedicated to edge devices, such as storage devices, can be variable in order to provide the required performance up to the maximum of the core. To achieve path redundancy, this topology uses multiple edge devices with connections to different core devices or highly available core ports. In the case of highly available switch ports, the same device will have port pairs designed to provide failover functions for each other.

4.6 Legacy Devices

Devices such as bridges can connect legacy devices—previously directly attached to host systems—to the new SAN. For example,

Fibre Channel–SCSI (FC-SCSI) bridges can connect older devices or devices that do not have a Fibre Channel interface to a SAN. FC-SCSI bridges provide conversion from parallel SCSI interfaces to the Fibre Channel interface. Any bridge can also connect older storage with critical data that is too difficult or costly to move to the new SAN.

Some devices that do not require high-performance connections have not yet been converted for use with a Fibre Channel interface. For example, manufacturers have not converted some types of tape drives. Therefore, many NAS replacement SANs for backups must use bridges to connect the tape drives to the SAN. The tape drives can then be allocated to host systems on the SAN as needed. The bridge improves the utilization of the tape drives, because they can be re-allocated to different host systems instead of sitting idle on a system with directly attached tape drives and no backup jobs to perform.

Bridges are effective for connecting groups of SCSI devices on one or more chains to a SAN fabric, making deployment of the devices more flexible. All SCSI devices are suitable for use with bridges, and support for all current SCSI types is available. Many different devices in addition to Fibre Channel devices can be connected to a SAN fabric using bridges.

4.7 Data Migration

In most cases, when converting an existing system from DAS access to SAN fabric storage access, data needs to be migrated from the old storage devices to the new ones. Migrating an existing application to SAN-based systems also requires moving data to those systems unless the data on the old and new systems can be joined in some way, or the old data can be ignored.

When changing storage devices, you can accomplish data migration with system or application tools. The migration requires a short period of time during which both old and new storage devices are connected to the new host. The existing file systems can be re-created on the new storage and mounted in a temporary area on the host system that uses the migrated data. The data can be copied to the file systems on the new storage devices using several methods, such as:

- Backup of the old devices with the restore target set to the new devices

- Recursive copy with the old file systems as the source and the new file systems as the target

EXAMPLE 4.1.   Using *dump* and *restore* for backup

```
dump -10 /oldfilesystem - | (cd /newfilesystem; restore - )
```

Backups can move data more effectively and preserve metadata such as file ownership. Example 4.1 shows a typical command that performs a backup of a single file system on a UNIX operating system.

This command streams data from the *dump* command on the old file system to the *restore* command that writes it to the new file system. Running multiple simultaneous instances of this command achieves maximum performance.

Note: When using the recursive copy method or the dump/restore method, the throughput of the system running the *dump* and *restore* commands is the only restriction on performance. Both of these migration methods use the system bus to transfer the data.

Migration of data to a new host system and new storage devices requires a recursive network copy or data transfer through an external backup and restore system. Use network file systems or a network-aware copy command such as the UNIX *rcp* command. In a network file system such as NFS, the dump/restore method can be performed as if local but with lower performance than when using local devices. Use the command in Example 4.1 with a network file system as the target.

If the bandwidth of the network link between the source and target sites is low, then migrating data with a backup system will take less time than a network copy. The data can be stored on removable media, shipped to the remote site, and restored to complete the migration of the data. After completing the restore, any changes made during the shipment of the media can then be copied over the slow network link to bring the remote system up to date. The use of backup media greatly reduces the time required to migrate the data, and it also reduces the amount of data sent over the slow network link.

Applications with proprietary data storage formats (such as an RDBMS using raw disk devices instead of file systems) can also migrate data using the dump/restore method. Applications with native dump/restore tools must be examined to see whether they can use a file system for the target dump device. The file system methods described above can migrate the data dumped from the application, and an application-specific restore can then be performed when the backup image of the data arrives at the remote site.

In most cases, data migration from old devices to new devices does not require more than a momentary application outage. During the entire time of data migration, the old data storage remains in use. Furthermore, the data can also be verified prior to the application switch to the new storage. The application need be stopped only long enough to switch the data devices it is addressing from the old devices to the new devices. Then new data created during the copy can be migrated from the now static, old storage devices to the new storage devices. If problems with the application occur, then a second short application outage is necessary to restart the old devices.

Now the migration process can be examined to determine why the application using the data on the new devices does not work. Data migrations using these methods are reliable and have minimal risk.

4.8 Summary

The guidelines for selecting SAN components, as well as the discussion of topology, presented in this chapter will inform your choice of devices and physical layouts as you carry out SAN projects. The methods for accommodating legacy devices and performing data migration described here will enable a smooth transition from old application complexes to new ones using SANs.

The next step: the physical integration and configuration of the SAN design.

5

SAN CONFIGURATION AND TESTING

The configuration and testing of a SAN needs to be carefully planned and executed in order to ensure a working implementation of the SAN design. A SAN design needs to be physically built and configured to support the application targeted for the SAN. All hardware and software features must be configured according to the design specification and then verified for correctness. Verification of the implementation against the design is performed with checklists and configuration management for the hardware, and with I/O model tests for the software and application behaviors.

5.1 Topologies for SAN Types

The topologies in this section are a standard set that most SAN applications can work with. Relying on standard topologies not only simplifies the deployment and management of SANs, but it also allows you to plan more accurately and set more realistic expectations for SAN deployment.

NAS Replacement SAN

For this example, we use the flat topology described in Chapter 4 (see page 99), which provides a simple hardware layout for the switch devices and meets the connectivity requirements of the devices. The required performance is not extreme, so the limitations of the flat topology are not a problem. Because there are only two fabric devices in this configuration, redundant connections to each switch from all of the devices can eliminate potential single points of failure. A single ISL can provide an in-band management connection between the SAN fabric devices.

The designer now translates the physical configuration to a cabling plan for physical assembly, as specified in Tables 5.1 and 5.2. The cabling plan defines the mapping of physical cable endpoints to available switch devices, host systems, and storage device ports. The plan lists each switch device with connectivity defined between specific ports and other devices, based on a logical set of two rules.

1. To derive a cabling plan, start by placing ISLs on the lowest numbered switch port available and work upward to the total of the required ISLs.

2. Then work downward from the highest numbered ports available for device connections that are not ISLs.

This cabling rule set is shown in Figure 5.1.

Storage Consolidation SAN

The storage consolidation SAN uses a two-tier topology for the fabric. This SAN uses four Fibre Channel switches to provide the required performance and connectivity. The host system tier and the storage device tier each have two devices. Four ISLs between the tiers provide the necessary bandwidth and redundancy for the SAN. In their respective tiers, the host systems and storage devices are also redundantly connected to each Fibre Channel switch.

TABLE 5.1. NAS Replacement SAN: Switch 1 Cabling Plan

Port ID	Remote Device Connection
Port 0	Switch 2, port 0
Port 1	Host 1, HBA 1
Port 2	Host 2, HBA 1
Port 3	Host 3, HBA 1
Port 4	Host 4, HBA 1
Port 5	Host 5, HBA 1
Port 6	Host 6, HBA 1
Port 7	Host 7, HBA 1
Port 8	Host 8, HBA 1
Port 9	Storage device 1, I/O channel 1
Port 10	Storage device 2, I/O channel 1
Port 11	Empty
Port 12	Empty
Port 13	Empty
Port 14	Empty
Port 15	Empty

TABLE 5.2. NAS Replacement SAN: Switch 2 Cabling Plan

Port ID	Remote Device Connection
Port 0	Switch 1, port 0
Port 1	Host 1, HBA 2
Port 2	Host 2, HBA 2
Port 3	Host 3, HBA 2
Port 4	Host 4, HBA 2
Port 5	Host 5, HBA 2
Port 6	Host 6, HBA 2
Port 7	Host 7, HBA 2
Port 8	Host 8, HBA 2
Port 9	Storage device 1, I/O channel 2
Port 10	Storage device 2, I/O channel 2
Port 11	Empty
Port 12	Empty
Port 13	Empty
Port 14	Empty
Port 15	Empty

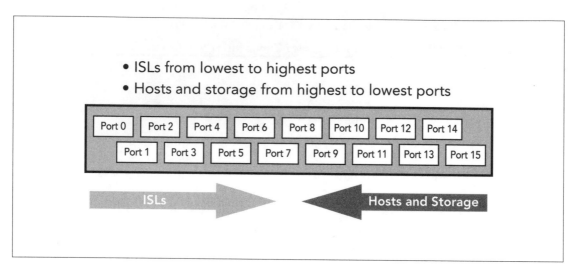

FIGURE 5.1

Basic Fibre Channel switch cabling rules

The cabling plan for this SAN, as specified in Tables 5.3 through 5.6, is somewhat complex, but the low number of total devices makes this a manageable configuration to implement.

Capacity-Planning SAN

The capacity-planning SAN also uses a two-tiered topology, because it is an effective configuration for device layout. It minimizes the required number of connections and isolates the types of connectivity in the SAN to local areas of fabric devices, storage devices, and host systems. Each of the two tiers has four switches. This configuration provides the connectivity required and a significant amount of expansion capability. Twenty-five percent of the installed ports remain available for additional connectivity. The SAN requires at least eight ISLs between the tiers to meet the combined expected performance requirements of the host systems. But twice that many ISLs must be used to connect the tiers. ISLs provide overhead for rising utilization due to the addition of host systems or storage devices.

TABLE 5.3. Storage Consolidation SAN: Switch 1 Cabling Plan

Port ID	Remote Device Connection
Port 0	Switch 3, port 0
Port 1	Switch 4, port 1
Port 2	Host 1, HBA 1
Port 3	Host 2, HBA 1
Port 4	Host 3, HBA 1
Port 5	Empty
Port 6	Empty
Port 7	Empty
Port 8	Empty
Port 9	Empty
Port 10	Empty
Port 11	Empty
Port 12	Empty
Port 13	Empty
Port 14	Empty
Port 15	Empty

TABLE 5.4. Storage Consolidation SAN: Switch 2 Cabling Plan

Port ID	Remote Device Connection
Port 0	Switch 4, port 0
Port 1	Switch 3, port 1
Port 2	Host 1, HBA 2
Port 3	Host 2, HBA 2
Port 4	Host 3, HBA 2
Port 5	Empty
Port 6	Empty
Port 7	Empty
Port 8	Empty
Port 9	Empty
Port 10	Empty
Port 11	Empty
Port 12	Empty
Port 13	Empty
Port 14	Empty
Port 15	Empty

TABLE 5.5.   Storage Consolidation SAN: Switch 3 Cabling Plan

Port ID	Remote Device Connection
Port 0	Switch 1, port 0
Port 1	Switch 2, port 1
Port 2	Storage device 1, I/O channel 1
Port 3	Storage device 2, I/O channel 1
Port 4	Storage device 3, I/O channel 1
Port 5	Storage device 4, I/O channel 1
Port 6	Storage device 5, I/O channel 1
Port 7	Storage device 6, I/O channel 1
Port 8	Empty
Port 9	Empty
Port 10	Empty
Port 11	Empty
Port 12	Empty
Port 13	Empty
Port 14	Empty
Port 15	Empty

TABLE 5.6.   Storage Consolidation SAN: Switch 4 Cabling Plan

Port ID	Remote Device Connection
Port 0	Switch 2, port 0
Port 1	Switch 1, port 1
Port 2	Storage device 1, I/O channel 2
Port 3	Storage device 2, I/O channel 2
Port 4	Storage device 3, I/O channel 2
Port 5	Storage device 4, I/O channel 2
Port 6	Storage device 5, I/O channel 2
Port 7	Storage device 6, I/O channel 2
Port 8	Empty
Port 9	Empty
Port 10	Empty
Port 11	Empty
Port 12	Empty
Port 13	Empty
Port 14	Empty
Port 15	Empty

The host systems and storage devices connect to the fabric through redundant switch connections that also meet the host system's performance requirements. The cabling plan for the capacity-planning SAN is complex, as specified in Tables 5.7 through 5.10. The plan must have independent physical verification when the assembly is complete, in order to avoid problems due to an improper integration, such as a failure to create proper redundant data paths. An auditor can use the cable plan to verify the proper physical layout of the SAN by simply creating a checklist for the cabling.

New Project SAN

The topology for a new project SAN is difficult to select because confidence in the performance and feature requirements may be low. As a good rule of thumb, base the topology on the expected number of devices requiring connections to the SAN. A configuration with a low number of connections and modest performance

TABLE 5.7. Capacity-Planning SAN: Switch 1 Cabling Plan

Port ID	Remote Device Connection
Port 0	Switch 3, port 0
Port 1	Switch 3, port 1
Port 2	Switch 4, port 2
Port 3	Switch 4, port 3
Port 4	Empty
Port 5	Empty
Port 6	Empty
Port 7	Empty
Port 8	Host 4, HBA 2
Port 9	Host 4, HBA 1
Port 10	Host 3, HBA 2
Port 11	Host 3, HBA 1
Port 12	Host 2, HBA 2
Port 13	Host 2, HBA 1
Port 14	Host 1, HBA 2
Port 15	Host 1, HBA 1

TABLE 5.8.   Capacity-Planning SAN: Switch 2 Cabling Plan

Port ID	Remote Device Connection
Port 0	Switch 4, port 0
Port 1	Switch 4, port 1
Port 2	Switch 3, port 2
Port 3	Switch 3, port 3
Port 4	Empty
Port 5	Empty
Port 6	Empty
Port 7	Empty
Port 8	Host 4, HBA 4
Port 9	Host 4, HBA 3
Port 10	Host 3, HBA 4
Port 11	Host 3, HBA 3
Port 12	Host 2, HBA 4
Port 13	Host 2, HBA 3
Port 14	Host 1, HBA 4
Port 15	Host 1, HBA 3

TABLE 5.9.   Capacity-Planning SAN: Switch 3 Cabling Plan

Port ID	Remote Device Connection
Port 0	Switch 1, port 0
Port 1	Switch 1, port 1
Port 2	Switch 2, port 2
Port 3	Switch 2, port 3
Port 4	Empty
Port 5	Empty
Port 6	Empty
Port 7	Empty
Port 8	Storage device 4, I/O channel 2
Port 9	Storage device 4, I/O channel 1
Port 10	Storage device 3, I/O channel 2
Port 11	Storage device 3, I/O channel 1
Port 12	Storage device 2, I/O channel 2
Port 13	Storage device 2, I/O channel 1
Port 14	Storage device 1, I/O channel 2
Port 15	Storage device 1, I/O channel 1

TABLE 5.10. Capacity-Planning SAN: Switch 4 Cabling Plan

Port ID	Remote Device Connection
Port 0	Switch 2, port 0
Port 1	Switch 2, port 1
Port 2	Switch 1, port 2
Port 3	Switch 1, port 3
Port 4	Empty
Port 5	Empty
Port 6	Empty
Port 7	Empty
Port 8	Storage device 4, I/O channel 4
Port 9	Storage device 4, I/O channel 3
Port 10	Storage device 3, I/O channel 4
Port 11	Storage device 3, I/O channel 3
Port 12	Storage device 2, I/O channel 4
Port 13	Storage device 2, I/O channel 3
Port 14	Storage device 1, I/O channel 4
Port 15	Storage device 1, I/O channel 3

expectations can easily use a star or flat topology. If the number of connections required for devices and host systems is less than the total number of ports in one or two typical Fibre Channel switches in the SAN, these topologies are fine. A larger number of connections than the number of ports in two typical Fibre Channel switches requires more complex tiered or full mesh topologies. These guidelines provide a reasonable set of starting assumptions when selecting the SAN topology for a new project.

Experimental SAN

The topology for an experimental SAN can be anything at all. It is an advantage to use topologies that are likely to be deployed in the production SAN. If possible, conduct experiments with the topology to help assess how a SAN will behave and perform when it is expanded in an unplanned or non-ideal way. These experiments provide a better idea of what to expect from a SAN when devices are added or removed in the ad hoc fashion that most production environments require.

5.2 Zoning, LUN Masking, and LUN Allocation

In a SAN, all devices have access to one another unless the configuration tools make a logical separation that segregates the devices. The zoning of a SAN provides this logical separation. Zoning prevents improper access either by accident or by malicious intent. The partitioning of devices into logical groupings creates smaller, more manageable device sets from the entire population of devices in the SAN. These sets, no matter how they are created and managed, are considered to be zones.

Planning for Zones

The logical grouping of SAN devices into zones can be based on several different components of the SAN:

- Host system
- Storage device
- Fabric device
- HBA

It is common for more than one logical grouping to be used in a single SAN that uses a storage device or SAN feature in addition to basic fabric connectivity.

HOST SYSTEM

Host system–based zones are convenient if the path to storage devices and the specific LUN allocations are not important. The LUNs or storage devices allocated to a host system are visible on all of the HBAs on that host system. This configuration is useful for implementing multiple I/O paths to the same storage device LUNs for failover and load balancing of I/O. The host-based zone configuration is problematic if large numbers of LUNs or storage devices are configured on a single host system. In this case, each access path multiplies the number of visible devices that must be managed. The host system–based configuration may also be difficult to use if the path to storage devices or LUNs is important for performance reasons. This difficulty arises because host-based zones allow the automatic fabric mechanisms to select the path that data takes when traversing the SAN.

STORAGE DEVICE

A storage device–based zone configuration is useful for shared storage devices that can have variable access to host systems. For example, tape devices used for backups on many different systems can be zoned in this way to ease the temporary deployment of a group of backup devices to multiple host systems. Alternatively, the devices in an entire tape robot can be moved from host system to host system by modifying the zone to include the host system currently being backed up. A storage device–based zone configuration is used in addition to another type of zone configuration in most SANs because it is difficult to provide complete device access control without additional logical device separation.

FABRIC DEVICE

Fabric device zones temporarily separate a single SAN into more than one group of devices that do not usually communicate. The core devices of a core-and-edge SAN topology can be separated into a zone that excludes the edge devices in order to allow a generic communication path not needed by the edge devices. The creation of core zones can be useful for restriction of access paths so that failure diagnosis and performance behaviors are more deterministic. Without core zones, the edge fabric devices can use any path to move data across the SAN core. The challenge created by core zones is maintenance of the multipath access nature of the high-performance core while reducing the number of paths and devices that data can use to cross the SAN.

HBA

An HBA-based zone creates the connection between a host system and the storage device that the host system addresses with a specific controller. This zone type creates the access path from the host system to the storage device by putting the endpoint ports of the SAN together. An HBA-based zone configuration has more zones, but the zones are in a more easily managed hierarchy. The HBAs in a host connect to storage device ports, and then the LUNs attached to the storage device ports are logically attached to the host through the HBA. This logical path—from host system to HBA, to storage device, to LUN—is easy to manage and understand when you are examining the configuration. HBA-based zones are the most general type of zone and should have the fewest number of entities to manage per zone. However, these zones can result in a higher number of zones per SAN.

Implementing Zones

Zone implementations combine identifiers of the zone endpoints into groups that can access each other through the fabric devices. The endpoint identifiers are usually device world-wide names (WWNs) or unique fabric device ports. The implementation and configuration of zones is specific to the type of fabric device used to build the SAN, but many devices have similar methods for zone creation.

The port-based implementation is easiest to use and implement because it requires knowledge of only the specific device-to-port connections. There is no logical difference between a port and what is attached to a port, so complex endpoints can be connected in a very simple way. If the paths are not explicitly specified, the fabric devices themselves derive the paths among endpoints using the Fibre Channel Shortest Path First (FSPF) standard. In general it is a good idea to let the SAN fabric devices self-configure data paths and then to address any problematic data path imbalances if they occur at all.

When the configuration uses a WWN identifier for zoning, then the fabric devices rely on the Simple Name Server (SNS) standard to make the fabric devices aware of all WWNs in the SAN. Each fabric switch device keeps a list of locally attached devices and exchanges that information with the other fabric switch devices connected to it. This process propagates a complete set of WWN information to the whole SAN. Other entities in the SAN, such as LUN-masking software, can also use the WWN information to control and access the devices.

The most difficult problem with WWN-based zoning occurs when devices fail and are replaced, because WWNs are device specific. A swapped device adds a new WWN to the SAN and removes a known WWN. The new device performs the same function as the replaced device, using a different WWN. The old WWN is in the old zone and the new one is not. At best, this does not create access problems and requires only an update of the appropriate zones. In the worst case, the storage device or host system affected by the new WWN becomes corrupted by an improper access or becomes unavailable for I/O.

Fabric devices that implement port-to-port or WWN-based zones generally cannot control access to LUNs in storage devices with an association to a specific port. The control of LUN access must currently be performed by another device in the SAN.

LUN masking provides control over a host system LUN access by preventing problematic access from a storage device or host system. For example, a switch device that implements port fanout requires control of LUN access. This configuration presents many LUNs from a single storage device port to multiple fanout ports on a fabric device. The fabric device is capable of access control only over the port where the LUNs are presented, not to the actual LUNs. The LUN-masking solution then creates access controls for the host systems accessing the LUNs on the shared storage device port.

Zoning can be used as a coarse type of LUN masking. If LUNs within a storage device can be allocated to a single port within that storage device, then port zoning can be used to accomplish LUN masking. To control access to LUNs that are allocated to only a single storage device port, create zones that include only the port and the HBA that will access those devices.

A software relationship in the LUN masking tool or device logically connects the WWN of the host system HBA to the LUNs attached to a specific port. Storage devices or host HBAs will consult the LUN-masking tool or device to determine device access. The LUN-masking tool or device is critical to the operation of the SAN and the systems on it, so the tool or device must be extremely reliable. Otherwise, device corruption may occur, lowering SAN availability and creating a significant recovery workload.

5.3 SAN-Specific Feature Deployment

Some SAN features require zone configurations or specific physical layouts to accommodate the functionality being deployed. At least one of the basic SAN topologies should accommodate any SAN-specific feature. The zone configuration is more likely to require adjustment in order to enable the functioning of a SAN feature in one of the basic topologies. Data replication through the SAN requires a zone that contains both endpoints of the replication in addition to any other zones that provide access to the data, in order to isolate the replication data traffic. The data traffic isolation is important for replication reliability. This type of zone contains the ports in replicated storage devices that have the allocated source and target LUNs. This zone has the effect of connecting the source and target LUNs with a direct logical path, even though the physical path may include many hops.

A data-sharing SAN also requires a specific sharing zone in addition to any other zones used for storage connectivity. The shared storage device in the configuration needs to be in a zone with all of the host system HBAs that will share the storage. In a SAN that uses Fibre Channel IP networking, the IP data traffic should be logically isolated from the storage data traffic. The logical separation of the SAN into an IP data network and a storage data network allows a more deterministic behavior for each type of traffic, which simplifies management and deployment. The separation of the data traffic types also enables more effective diagnosis of any SAN problems.

The goal of a SAN feature-specific zone is to isolate the connectivity required for the feature. Isolating the data paths used for the SAN feature in addition to the storage connectivity paths simplifies the configuration and management of the feature and the SAN. The SAN feature-specific zone reduces the number of devices, LUNs, and HBAs to the minimum required for the feature to function properly. The feature-specific zone also reduces confusion in the SAN fabric because the logical connections replace the physical ones with respect to connectivity.

5.4 Application-Specific Fabric Configuration

An application that is SAN aware also requires a specific zone in order to isolate it from the rest of the SAN. SAN application-specific zones are possible in any SAN topology. The topology and the SAN-aware application are usually complementary, so that the creation of an application-specific zone can easily be accommodated by the physical and logical SAN layout.

A data transfer application requires the endpoints that enable the data transfer to be in a zone together. The devices that are the source and target for the data, as well as any middleman devices for data translation, all need to be in the same zone for the data transfer to occur. If two host systems transfer data through a storage device in a client/server fashion, with the storage performing the metadata translation, then the host system HBAs and the storage device ports with the necessary LUNs for the application all need to be in the same zone. A SAN backup application requires application-specific zones for the host systems being backed up. The backup devices and storage devices being backed up must be in the same zone in order to provide the data connectivity required for the backup application.

When using direct SAN access to transfer data, the ports in the storage devices attached to the LUNs being backed up and the backup devices performing the backups must be in the same zone while backups are performed. The configuration also requires additional zones to simplify the addition and removal of backup devices and storage devices from zones. Simplifying zone changes enables the backup SAN to be more flexible and perform more backups on multiple host systems, while keeping the host systems isolated from each other.

The goal of application-specific zones is the same as that of SAN feature-specific zones: both isolate traffic in order to simplify the configuration and functionality of the SAN. The difference is in the level of isolation and the functional requirements. The application-level zones are a logical level above the SAN feature-specific zones, even though they are both implemented in the same way.

Zones enable connectivity only in the most basic way. Beyond simple connectivity, zones provide isolation for specific data traffic types. Also, they enable functionality for applications by removing physical connection limitations from devices that would have these limitations under normal configuration circumstances.

5.5 A Complete SAN

A capacity-planning SAN combines many features of the other SAN types into a single project, so it is helpful to examine the complete implementation of a capacity-planning SAN in detail. The requirements for a capacity-planning SAN intended to support data warehouse and ETL applications include:

- Eight host systems of two different types to support all necessary applications

- Data-sharing software that requires a dedicated host system

- 800MB/s of aggregate fabric bandwidth

- Connectivity for SCSI tape devices

- Storage device–based block data replication

- Eight 1.5TB intelligent storage systems used to provide 12TB of storage space

- Redundant connectivity for all devices to enable multipath I/O

The requirements are set by examining the applications and host systems for compatibility and I/O behaviors, selecting storage devices with a desired feature set, and identifying specific SAN features desired. The I/O assessment tools in Chapter 3 are used to evaluate host systems performing tasks similar to the applications that are expected to be deployed on the capacity-planning SAN. The storage devices are commonly used components in this environment that are the appropriate size and contain the data replication feature.

The SAN data-sharing software is desirable because it improves the performance of the applications by reducing the number of file transfer operations. The data-sharing software is selected by evaluating the available products and choosing the right one for this environment. The selection criteria for this software are the following:

- Host type for running data-sharing software

- Storage device compatibility with data-sharing software

- Data-sharing software client compatibility

The SAN uses a tiered topology to connect the storage devices and host systems to one another with a Fibre Channel fabric. The aggregate fabric bandwidth is the total bandwidth if all of the ISLs are in use at the same time. The core of the fabric must be made up of a minimum of eight ISLs. Switches should be the fabric devices used for the SAN tiers because the bandwidth demands on the fabric are high. If a sixteen-port switch device is used, then four switches are capable of providing the thirty-two edge ports for host system and storage device connectivity, in addition to the sixteen interior ISL ports, the two data-sharing server host system ports, and the two SCSI bridge ports. There are eight remaining ports throughout the fabric for additional connectivity if necessary. The connection of additional devices should be evaluated carefully, because the SAN has been sized with specific requirements: any additional load can cause problems. Figure 5.2 shows the complete SAN and component connections.

5.6 Testing

If possible, test the new storage devices with the applications and data in place. The tests should attempt to verify data availability as well as expected SAN performance. Testing the SAN also helps to uncover any oddities or improper configurations. Finally, a tested SAN provides more deterministic results for the host systems and applications that use the SAN for storage access.

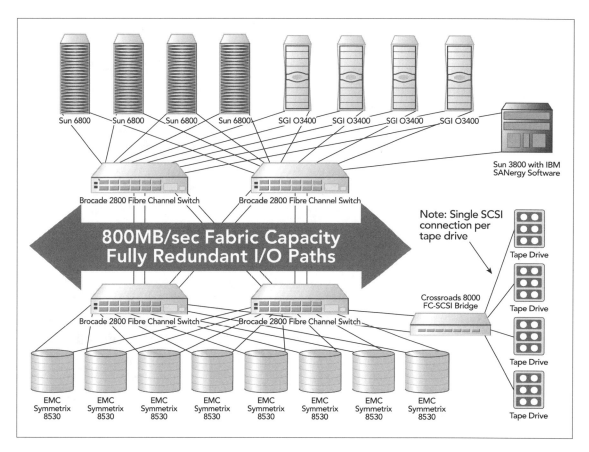

FIGURE 5.2

Data warehouse and ETL application capacity-planning SAN

Typical tests include:

- Simulation of the peak and typical measurements from the application analysis and I/O behavior assessment using the models developed in Chapter 3

- Several runs of each test to ensure consistent test results

- Verification of the SAN using the I/O behaviors and performance envelopes of the applications and host systems

NAS Replacement SAN

In the NAS replacement SAN, testing should verify the data access availability and SAN bandwidth performance. Multiple files should be concurrently written to the SAN-based file system. Those files should then be concurrently read by multiple systems. This testing simulates the access patterns observed during the I/O assessment and the behaviors expected of the new SAN features. These simulations provide a baseline set of expectations for SAN behavior and a performance comparison with the production systems at deployment.

Storage Consolidation SAN

Testing of the storage consolidation SAN uses models developed from the assessment of the systems being consolidated. The model used for testing the storage consolidation SAN combines the measured performance and behaviors of the existing systems. A single model that combines all the existing host system and application behaviors is difficult to develop. A concurrent run of multiple host system models or application models is a good method for testing the combined workload of the consolidated host systems and applications. The observed behaviors under testing allow for modifications to the SAN if the workload combination is discovered to cause unexpected behaviors.

Capacity-Planning SAN

The SAN for capacity planning is difficult to test due to the unknown application and I/O behaviors. Testing can verify the design specifications and I/O behaviors of the most probable applications targeted for deployment. The tests set expectations for application deployment.

Testing of the capacity-planning SAN uses the typical application data sets or at least data sets that have sizes and data types in common with typical applications. The access methods simulated can be combinations of several applications or several instances of a single application. Both types of testing can be done if time and resources allow it. Examination of the most common application usage in your environment determines the types of tests to combine. This testing enables the reasonable setting of expectations for I/O behaviors and performance of applications deployed on the capacity-planning SAN.

New Project SAN

Testing verifies that a new project SAN supports the needs of the new project. Models that simulate the workload of existing systems, and applications that are somewhat like the new project, can verify performance expectations and application I/O behavior. This testing provides only a basic understanding of the SAN behaviors under a likely workload. To make the best assessment possible, testing of the new project SAN should include testing of the new project workload.

Experimental SAN

The sole purpose of an experimental SAN is testing. This testing examines the SAN I/O behaviors of interest as thoroughly as possible. Models that drive extreme bandwidth, IOPS, and combinations of the two should be used to investigate the SAN as a whole and its individual components. Many variables can be changed to examine the effect on basic tests and data access. These variables include:

- I/O size

- Number of access paths through the fabric

- HBA tunable parameters

- Storage device tunable parameters

- System tunable parameters

The tests run on the experimental SAN provide a good set of expectations for SANs of all types at deployment of a production SAN.

5.7 Summary

Testing an implemented SAN to compare the measurements of I/O behavior and performance to existing systems without SAN-based storage is extremely valuable for evaluating a SAN deployment. The validation of the SAN that testing provides will raise the confidence level of customers using the SAN. The physical installation and logical configuration of a SAN can be the most difficult part of a SAN project due to the complexity. The thorough cable plans and configuration rules described in this chapter will make this task manageable. Now the day-to-day operations of a SAN can be considered, which we will do in Chapter 6.

6

SAN CONTROL AND MONITORING

After a SAN has been designed and physically integrated, a significant amount of work remains to configure the devices and ensure that they function as expected. Tools for management and configuration are available from several sources, and they can also be created in-house. Tools for event and performance monitoring are critical to the continued proper functioning of a SAN on a day-to-day basis. The effective selection of tools for SAN management and monitoring creates a SAN environment where the tools enable simple diagnosis of problems that occur. Good SAN tools can also facilitate reconfiguration with minimal effort and integration into the online functions of applications using the SAN.

6.1 Management Tools

The task of managing a SAN is an ongoing process. Events and changes that affect a SAN occur due to normal use of the SAN, as well as device failures or configuration anomalies. All of these occurrences must be corrected or dealt with in some way. Failures must be repaired immediately, and if possible, changes should be planned to minimize disruption of the SAN.

There are a number of SAN management methods and tools. Currently no single tool provides complete end-to-end management methods on a SAN for all possible devices that may be used. Off-the-shelf tools cover most common host systems, HBAs, fabric devices, and storage devices, but no single tool provides enough features unless the SAN environment is extremely homogeneous. It is likely that several different tools will need to be combined.

The best choice for SAN management is a combination of off-the-shelf tools and in-house tools that are built specifically to operate in your environment. The off-the-shelf tools selected should be able to provide information about, and allow management of, as many SAN devices as possible. If using more than one off-the-shelf tool, be prepared to create a middleware tool that combines the output from the purchased tools in a meaningful way. Otherwise, plan on using the tools separately, with less efficiency.

The most commonly combined data from a SAN is event data. This data is available from all SAN devices, generally in a documented format for each device. A SAN event is any SAN state change that may affect the performance or availability of the SAN or that may indicate an imminent problem. Informational events, such as the addition or removal of devices, may also be useful, but these events have a lower priority. Tools that collect SAN event data usually send it to a central console within the tool but do not report the data to an external source. In order to limit the number of consoles that need to be monitored, it is extremely useful to pick a single central entity for event data reporting. The data-reporting entity can be any tool as long as all of the other tools can report their information to the one chosen.

Tools that are developed in-house to fill gaps in the coverage of off-the-shelf tools should also be able to report events to the central event tool. The most common mechanisms for event reporting, such as e-mail directly from devices and SNMP, are available to extract and process events in most cases from most devices. E-mail events are generated when a device that supports e-mail detects a state change or other condition, and then sends an e-mail message to an address previously specified in the device configuration.

All devices that provide a management or monitoring interface can be maintained effectively through central event reporting. The central reporting of events can have a consistent look and feel that makes SAN management much easier. Reporting the event data to a redundant system through an alternate channel will also be extremely useful. For example, a fabric device can send an error message to the central event tool and an e-mail to the on-call SAN administrator. If one notification method fails, the other provides a backup.

SNMP

Almost all devices in a SAN will have an SNMP[1] agent available that can gather information about the device status and make configuration changes. Unmanaged devices such as hubs and Fibre-Channel-to-SCSI bridges do not generally have SNMP information available. However, unmanaged devices rarely have any software configuration ability or remote monitoring features, so lack of information is no great loss.

Devices that can be managed using SNMP will have a Management Information Base (MIB) that defines all of the possible information that can be gathered from the device. There are standard MIBs, developed by industry groups[2] and supported by many fabric devices, as well as device-specific MIBs. Combined, the standard industry MIBs and the device-specific MIBs make up the complete information set for an SNMP-aware fabric device.

Host systems and storage devices have agents that report SNMP information as well. The MIBs for host systems and storage devices

---

1. See http://www.snmpworld.com for more detailed information on SNMP.

2. Industry groups working on SAN MIBs include the Fibre Channel Industry Association (http://www.fibrechannel.com) and the Storage Network Industry Association (http://www.snia.org), among others.

also have standard and device-specific information sets that combine to give a complete picture of the status of the managed device.

The data gathered from the SNMP agents on the devices can be collected into a console that can represent the SAN information, either as a simple list of events and information or as a picture of the SAN and its status, if the tool is aware of the relations among the SAN devices. SNMP traps can be used to monitor alerts for devices in a SAN with an SNMP management console, even if the SNMP console is not SAN-aware. Any SNMP console can still use the MIB provided for a SAN device to manage traps and set off alarms when a trap event occurs.

Most SNMP management tools are designed with respect to IP network management and are a poor fit for anything more than SAN trap alerting. SNMP traps do not contain all the potentially useful event information that is available from SAN devices, so some other tools based on SNMP data extraction are useful if they can be obtained off the shelf or developed internally.

The SNMP module for the Perl programming language allows the extraction of arbitrary SNMP MIB information about any SNMP-aware device through a Perl script. This is extremely useful when creating tools that can allow more useful event management or monitoring for SAN devices. For example, the extraction of the data transmission error count on each port of a Fibre Channel switch can be used to discover potential SAN problems or component failures before they occur. This type of information does not normally cause an SNMP event until the device actually fails and causes an outage. So it is advantageous to gather the information and create a rule set for processing the SNMP information in addition to the simple MIB traps that SAN devices output. Data extracted using a script can also be stored in a generic database for usage trend analysis and capacity planning.

Other Network Tools

In addition to the SNMP tools, there may be vendor-specific out-of-band network tools for management. Out-of-band tools use a connection that is provided to the device in addition to the connection for data transfer. Out-of-band networks for Fibre Channel SANs are commonly IP networks in the same location as the SAN. These tools can be used to extract useful information that SNMP presents poorly or that the MIB provided does not include. Logs from devices are a good example of information that SNMP presents poorly. SNMP mechanisms do not work well for extracting a log of arbitrary length.

By providing access to devices in the SAN using an alternative method such as command line login or UNIX *syslogd* compatibility, management information can be extracted for evaluation without SNMP. Device logs can be sent to a host system using *syslogd*, and then the generated log file can be parsed for valuable information and events based on any rule set that your environment requires. Systems that allow access to a command line interface through a network interface can have the command line interaction scripted with simple tools like Perl or Expect[3] scripts that perform many useful management tasks. The command line access scripts can be used for configuration extraction and installation when changes need to be made to the SAN. The configuration information for SAN devices can also be extracted on a regular basis and compared with a known good configuration for change management, revision control purposes, and configuration drift prevention.

SAN devices that have networked service processors for management and monitoring can be managed the same way as devices that are accessed directly through a network connection. The networked service processor provides additional abstraction of the SAN device and offers connectivity for the device to a management IP network.

---

3. Expect is a tool written in the Tcl language to perform automated tasks that normally require challenge and response. Useful Expect information can be found at http://expect.nist.gov. A good Tcl resource is available at http://www.scriptics.com.

In the case of devices with a service processor, management interaction may be restricted to a single tool or method, but that tool or method can still be used to accomplish most tasks that can be performed over a network connection. The additional abstraction that the service processor presents is an aspect of certain SAN devices that requires attention and can likely be accommodated by any tool developed in-house.

Out-of-band network tools for SAN management are useful for the management of fabric devices that can be difficult to control using another facility or cannot provide necessary information in any other way. The tools used over a network connection must still be combined with any other tools to present a complete picture of the SAN and to provide effective control of devices.

In-Band Management Facilities

A common management method uses in-band connections to devices over the same channels that transfer data. The overhead is minimal, and the advantage of this management method is a lighter infrastructure requirement. Storage devices are commonly managed using this method because they have to be connected to host systems for data access. The in-band management method places some additional workload on the host system performing the management tasks for devices. Normally, management does not have a significant impact on the host system that is performing management tasks for SAN devices as well as running a production application.

In-band management of devices usually requires a device-specific agent or tool that runs on a host system connected to the managed device, to make device control requests through a device management mechanism, which is usually an API. For example, many storage devices have in-band management agents or tools that are simply processes on the host system. These agents maintain a connection to the storage device, in order to pass state information from the storage device to the host system and configuration information from the host system to the storage device when configuration changes are made. The agent or tool requires some host system CPU utilization, and it also needs to be compatible with the systems on the SAN performing the management tasks.

If the agent does not run on one of the host system types installed in the SAN, then a management-specific host system also needs to be connected to the SAN. This can create additional infrastructure and host systems management requirements that may make in-band management less desirable. A good example of this type of SAN management is the use of a Windows NT system to manage a SAN that supports UNIX systems as database servers. The Windows NT host system may create more management overhead for the host systems than the in-band management saves on the SAN.

In-band management is extremely dependent on the quality and reliability of the agent software used to perform the management tasks. If it is directly available to perform tasks, an agent or tool can affect the ability of the operators or administrators to automate and simplify SAN management tasks based on the tool's ease of use. In most cases, in-band mechanisms require additional work for the creation of tools that use the in-band management to perform useful tasks: the in-band mechanisms are mostly limited to interfaces to devices instead of being complete tools.

6.2 Management Consoles

SAN management consoles or SAN resource managers have been developed to manage SAN fabrics, the devices that make them up, and the host systems and storage devices that use the SAN. Management consoles generally perform at least one of several tasks that include topology discovery and visualization, LUN masking, LUN zoning, SAN event management, and SAN resource management.

Varying implementation methods and unevenness in supported devices available in these tools make their usability somewhat limited. A management console has to be used with a SAN consisting of only supported host systems, storage devices, and fabric devices; otherwise, the console will be limited to only partial awareness of the SAN. This limited awareness of the whole SAN leaves unknowns in the discovery and visualization that can lead to problems with access if the tool is performing LUN masking or LUN zoning tasks. Event and resource management is also limited to the known devices, making the management console a less than ideal tool for SANs with unsupported devices.

A SAN management console can be used effectively if the SAN design happens to be implemented with a completely supported set of devices for the selected console tool and the management console has all of the features required by the SAN applications. The range of choices for a SAN management console is currently very limited for heterogeneous SANs. The short-term prospects for SAN management consoles on homogeneous storage devices, host systems, and fabric switch SANs are better, but the right combination of supported devices and features may not exist in any off-the-shelf tool.

6.3 Event Monitoring

Events are state changes in the SAN or a device. Some events are informational, and others indicate device malfunctions that need to be remedied. Events within the SAN must be monitored in order to maintain the availability and reliability of critical applications.

Informational events do not indicate a failure condition, but in some cases they can be correlated to predict a future component failure. A good example of informational event correlation involves several recurring cooling fan messages from a Fibre Channel switch device. These messages indicate a low-RPM condition pointing to a likely failure of the fan in the near future. Some informational events are more difficult to correlate, and a component failure may occur that is different from the predicted one, but at least there is a good chance of performing preventive maintenance if the information is being evaluated.

Events can come from any device on the SAN, and these events must be gathered from SAN devices in multiple ways. Generally, the devices that need to be monitored for events are the fabric devices, the host systems, and the storage devices. Each one of these devices has its own specific method for reporting events, and each can have more than one event reporting method. Each of the devices can have SNMP traps defined in its MIB for event reporting to an SNMP trap console. The host systems have an internal log for events as well, such as *syslog* on UNIX systems. Windows NT systems can use installed third-party tools similar to *syslogd* or use the default Windows NT system logs. Storage devices may have a log file from a device management agent on the host system the storage devices are connected to, or an internal device log. Fabric devices also have management agent logs or internal device logs.

No matter how events are reported by the devices on a SAN, they should all be gathered and evaluated. An SNMP console can be used for SNMP trap gathering from all of the devices that use that method for event reporting. A simpler method involves the collection of device logs from each SAN device and the application of a rule set to the logs, using a log parsing tool that can perform actions or at least send notifications based on the event rules. There are several freeware tools that implement this log-parsing task, such as swatch[4] or logsurfer.[5] In-house tools are an option for parsing the logs as well.

The rule set used to perform actions and notifications is much more important than the tool used to apply the rules. The SAN event rule

---

4. See http://www.oit.ucsb.edu/~eta/swatch/ for details on swatch.

5. See http://www.cert.dfn.de/eng/logsurf/ for details on logsurfer.

set can be developed over time based on experiences with the SAN. At the start, all event messages can be mailed to the SAN administrator. As time goes on, the less critical messages can continue to be mailed to the SAN administrator or be ignored completely, while component failure or other highly critical messages can be sent directly to the on-call SAN administrator's pager for immediate response. Power supply failure messages from a Fibre Channel switch can be sent immediately as a page; data errors can be e-mailed to see if there is more than a single occurrence that can indicate a SAN problem. The more messages you receive, the better the rule set for handling the events becomes.

6.4 Performance Monitoring

Monitoring fabric device utilization and performance is important in order to maintain acceptable SAN behaviors and awareness of general SAN usage parameters. Monitoring the utilization of the SAN requires knowledge of the absolute capacity of the SAN fabric devices. The amount of SAN fabric device capacity in use by the host systems and storage devices on the SAN can be determined by comparing the measured usage of the fabric devices to the known capacity of host systems and storage devices.

One method of measuring the performance of the fabric devices involves extraction of per-port usage statistics from the fabric devices. These statistics give a port-by-port view of fabric device usage. By looking at all of the port statistics in a fabric device, administrators can get a complete picture of any fabric device. Then, by looking at all of the aggregated fabric devices on the SAN at once, admins can evaluate the SAN as a whole.

The most interesting usage statistic for fabric devices is the amount of data passing through each port, which is called the per-port bandwidth. This number can be extracted from all fabric devices by at least one method—and usually more than one—because most fabric devices will have a proprietary performance presentation tool as well as a standard data extraction method for performance data such as SNMP.

Use of SNMP makes a good start toward device performance data gathering, because it is a common management infrastructure component and implemented by many devices. Gather the performance data for fabric devices by examining the device MIB to find out what parameters to evaluate, and then polling the MIB object IDs of those parameters in order to collect their values periodically. Once the data is collected, it can be stored, visualized, and analyzed.

Storage of performance data can be as simple as appending the next value gathered into a flat file, or something more complex such as a database. There are many good data storage tools, so picking a familiar tool and using it for this purpose should be easy. SAN-aware management tools usually collect performance data as a part of the overall tool features, which also include the visualization and analysis of the gathered data. If you are not using a SAN-aware management tool, some form of database is best for storing performance data. A lot of data is required to get a good assessment of the SAN, so flat files can quickly become unmanageable. RRDtool[6] is a freeware tool that provides several useful features such as data visualization and data storage. The performance data can be stored, visualized, and extracted using a Perl interface or the tool components themselves.

SAN performance data should be visualized to assess the well-being of the SAN at a glance, because unusual behaviors, such as extremely high, sustained port bandwidth utilization, should be easily detected visually. Visual assessment of SAN performance can also detect configuration problems and other issues. Visualizing the aggregate performance of all of the ports in a fabric device enables

---

6. See http://www.rrdtool.com for details on RRDtool.

an immediate evaluation of fabric device utilization. If the visualization of aggregate performance shows a fabric device or the SAN to be close to its maximum throughput, then there is a need for some additional evaluation of the fabric device or SAN. There may be a requirement for additional capacity if all is as expected and the fabric device or SAN utilization is still high. If the high utilization appears abnormal, then there may also be a fabric device or SAN configuration problem.

Performance monitoring can clearly show a problem that may be causing more data to pass through a heavily used fabric switch than the switch has been configured to accommodate. If the inspection of a suspect fabric device shows data traffic to be abnormally high on some ports, there may be a zone configuration problem, component failure, or other problem that may not cause an event to be generated. These conditions cause the fabric device to work harder than it has been configured and sized to work. These conditions are also easily detectable with a quick look at the graph of any device's performance over time.

Periodic behaviors can also be detected by visualizing the SAN device performance data. These behaviors can be correlated with application behaviors on the host systems using the SAN. This correlation can then be used to adjust application job timings, if possible, to smooth out any peaks in the graphs and get more consistent SAN usage. The SAN visualization may also be used to help validate performance expectations such as absolute bandwidth demands, because this data is easily evaluated graphically.

The simple Perl script in Example 6.1 extracts SNMP data from a sixteen-port SAN fabric switch and stores it in an RRDtool archive. The script gathers the input-word and output-word counter values from the switch MIB for each port in a sixteen-port switch and then stores every value in an RRDtool archive. The input and output values can be combined to give the throughput of the port, and all of the ports can be combined to give the throughput of the entire switch.

EXAMPLE 6.1.   A Perl script for archiving (getswperf.pl)

```perl
#!/usr/local/bin/perl
#
# Get Fibre Channel switch performance
#
use RRDs;
use Net::SNMP;

$swname = "$ARGV[0]";

$switchperfpath = "/data/SANswitch/perf-stats/";

$i=1;
# Check each port in the switch for the number
# of Fibre Channel words transmitted.

while ( $i <= 16 ) {

    # SNMP parameter initialization
    ($session, $error) = Net::SNMP->session(
        -hostname  => "$swname",
        -community => "public",
        -port      =>  161
    );

    if (!defined($session)) {
        printf("ERROR: %s.\n", $error);
        exit 1;
    }

    # Grab the number of words transmitted and store it
    my $txcounter = "1.3.6.1.4.1.1588.2.1.1.1.6.2.1.11.$i";

    if (!defined($response = $session->get_request($txcounter))) {
        printf("ERROR: %s.\n", $session->error());
        $session->close();
        exit 1;
    }
```

EXAMPLE 6.1 (*continued*).   A Perl script for archiving (getswperf.pl)

```perl
    $txperf[$i] = $response->{$txcounter};

    $session->close();

    $i++;
}

$j=1;
# Check each port in the switch for the number
# of Fibre Channel words received.
while ( $j <= 16 ) {

    ($session, $error) = Net::SNMP->session(
        -hostname  => "$swname",
        -community => "public",
        -port      =>  161
    );

    if (!defined($session)) {
        printf("ERROR: %s.\n", $error);
        exit 1;
    }

    # Grab the number of words received and store it
    my $rxcounter = "1.3.6.1.4.1.1588.2.1.1.1.6.2.1.12.$j";

    if (!defined($response = $session->get_request($rxcounter))) {
        printf("ERROR: %s.\n", $session->error());
        $session->close();
        exit 1;
    }

    $rxperf[$j] = $response->{$rxcounter};

    $session->close();

    $j++;
}
```

EXAMPLE 6.1 (*continued*).   A Perl script for archiving (getswperf.pl)

```
# Add transmitted and received words together
# for total port performance
$k=1;
while ( $k <= 16 ) {
    $portperf[$k] = $rxperf[$k] + $txperf[$k];
    # Output the total performance of reach port
    printf "Port $k performance is $portperf[$k] \n";
    $k++;
}


# Store the port performance statistics in an
# RRDtool database

RRDs::update($switchperfpath.$swname.".".rrd,"N:$rxperf[1]:$txperf[1]:$rx
perf[2]:$txperf[2]:$rxperf[3]:$txperf[3]:$rxperf[4]:$txperf[4]:$rxperf[5]
:$txperf[5]:$rxperf[6]:$txperf[6]:$rxperf[7]:$txperf[7]:$rxperf[8]:$txper
f[8]:$rxperf[9]:$txperf[9]:$rxperf[10]:$txperf[10]:$rxperf[11]:$txperf[11
]:$rxperf[12]:$txperf[12]:$rxperf[13]:$txperf[13]:$rxperf[14]:$txperf[14]
:$rxperf[15]:$txperf[15]:$rxperf[16]:$txperf[16]");
my $ERR=RRDs::error;
die "ERROR while updating mydemo.rrd: $ERR\n" if $ERR;
```

Figure 6.1 shows the aggregate bandwidth usage of a typical Fibre Channel switch in the host tier of a SAN being used by two host systems for data warehousing. Figures 6.2 through 6.17 show the per-port bandwidth usage of the switch. We can see several useful things in these graphs. The total utilization of the fabric switch peaks at just under 300MB/s, so there is no shortfall of switch bandwidth because this switch should be capable of 800MB/s. The per-port throughput graphs in particular show that the majority of data traffic occurs on seven of the sixteen ports. This data isolation is consistent with the zoning configuration in use here, so there are no apparent configuration problems. Figure 6.10 shows a port bandwidth utilization that is at the maximum for the port for a short time, so some data access paths must be adjusted to remedy this if possible.

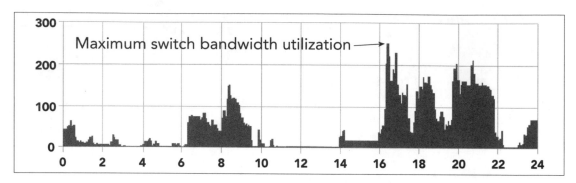

FIGURE 6.1

Aggregate Fibre Channel switch, 24-hour utilization, bandwidth (MB/s) versus time (hours)

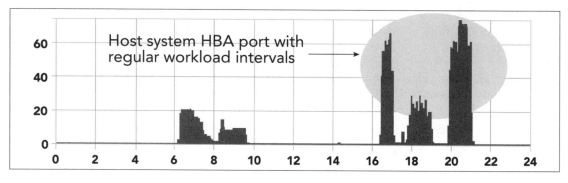

FIGURE 6.2

Fibre Channel switch port 0, 24-hour utilization, bandwidth (MB/s) versus time (hours)

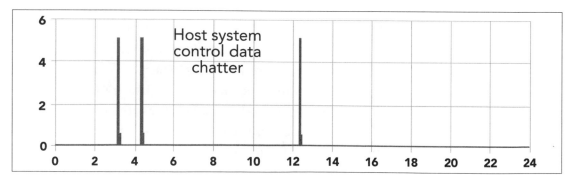

FIGURE 6.3

Fibre Channel switch port 1, 24-hour utilization, bandwidth (KB/s) versus time (hours)

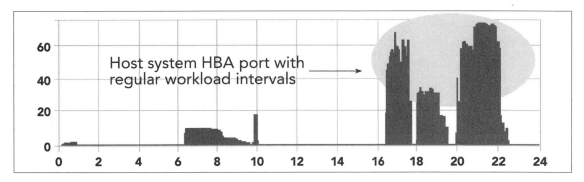

FIGURE 6.4

Fibre Channel switch port 2, 24-hour utilization, bandwidth (MB/s) versus time (hours)

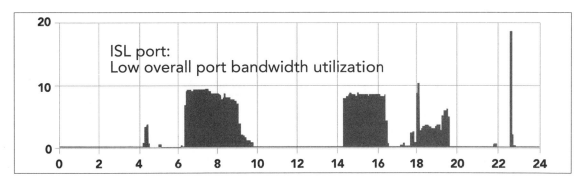

FIGURE 6.5

Fibre Channel switch port 3, 24-hour utilization, bandwidth (MB/s) versus time (hours)

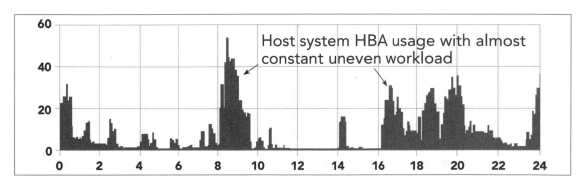

FIGURE 6.6

Fibre Channel switch port 4, 24-hour utilization, bandwidth (MB/s) versus time (hours)

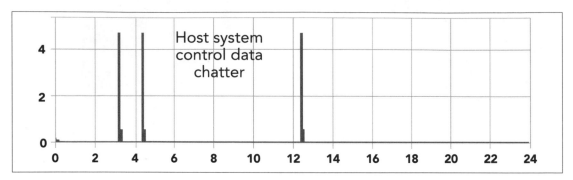

FIGURE 6.7

Fibre Channel switch port 5, 24-hour utilization, bandwidth (KB/s) versus time (hours)

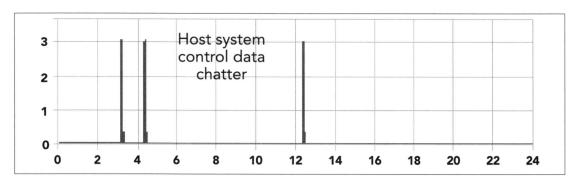

FIGURE 6.8

Fibre Channel switch port 6, 24-hour utilization, bandwidth (KB/s) versus time (hours)

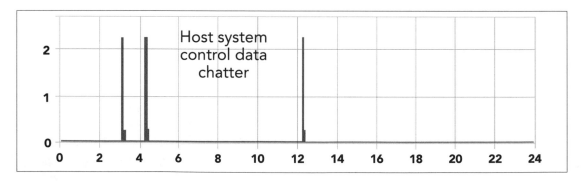

FIGURE 6.9

Fibre Channel switch port 7, 24-hour utilization, bandwidth (KB/s) versus time (hours)

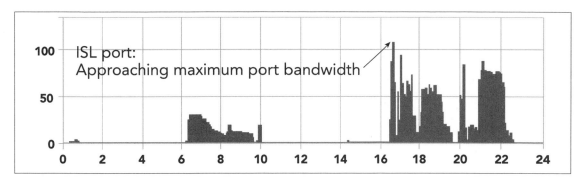

FIGURE 6.10

Fibre Channel switch port 8, 24-hour utilization, bandwidth (MB/s) versus time (hours)

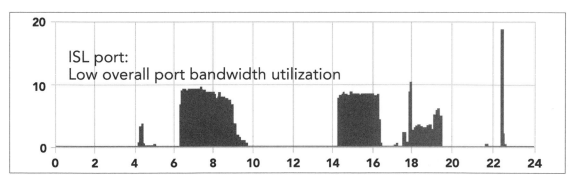

FIGURE 6.11

Fibre Channel switch port 9, 24-hour utilization, bandwidth (MB/s) versus time (hours)

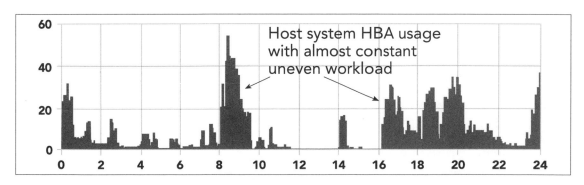

FIGURE 6.12

Fibre Channel switch port 10, 24-hour utilization, bandwidth (MB/s) versus time (hours)

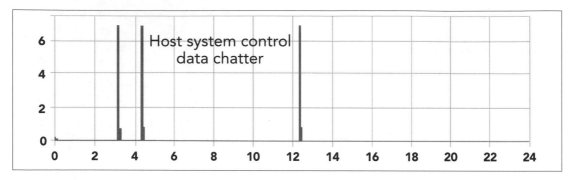

FIGURE 6.13

Fibre Channel switch port 11, 24-hour utilization, bandwidth (KB/s) versus time (hours)

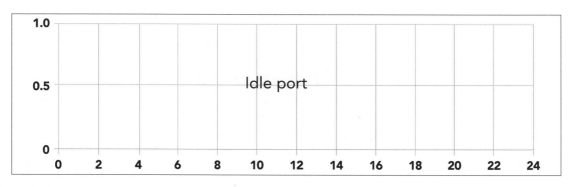

FIGURE 6.14

Fibre Channel switch port 12, 24-hour utilization, bandwidth (Bytes/s) versus time (hours)

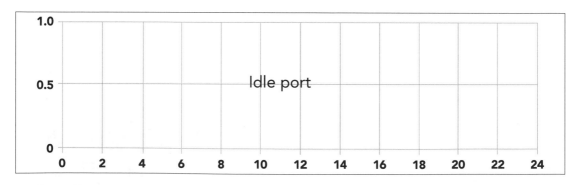

FIGURE 6.15

Fibre Channel switch port 13, 24-hour utilization, bandwidth (Bytes/s) versus time (hours)

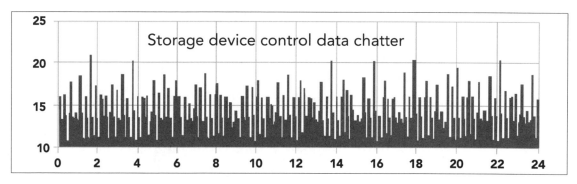

FIGURE 6.16

Fibre Channel switch port 14, 24-hour utilization, bandwidth (Bytes/s) versus time (hours)

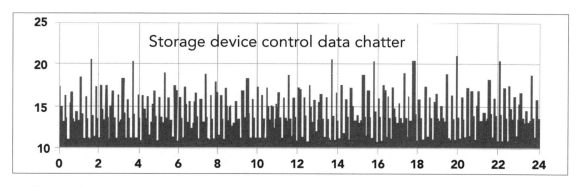

FIGURE 6.17

Fibre Channel switch port 15, 24-hour utilization, bandwidth (Bytes/s) versus time (hours)

SAN performance monitoring provides useful information about SAN activity and behavior. Reviewing SAN performance data on a regular basis helps with management of SAN growth and gives early warning of capacity problems. SAN performance monitoring also aids in the detection of SAN problems that event monitoring may not detect.

6.5 Fabric Zoning Reconfiguration as an Application

SAN fabric reconfiguration can be used to modify the SAN for a short time for the purpose of device reallocation. Shared storage devices can be presented to different systems on a SAN at different times by changing the SAN zoning configuration. Zoning changes to the fabric are a control function that requires a very stable set of tools and procedures if zone changes will be used dynamically in production. Configuration control is difficult because the fabric zones can be in one of several different states.

If the fabric device being used allows multiple zone configurations to be stored, then reconfiguration between any of the stored configurations requires a simple command or two. The current configuration is disabled and another configuration is enabled. To be of maximum use, applications and host systems must be able to add and remove devices without rebooting or restarting for zone reconfigurations.

If the fabric devices do not allow the storage of several zone configurations, then you must run the complete set of fabric device–specific commands to delete or disable an old configuration and to install a new one. Complete testing of the procedures and a step-by-step list of tasks is required to avoid problems when the SAN zone configuration is being changed several times per day in order to share devices. Fabric reconfiguration is poorly suited to automation, so it is likely to be successful only if it is deployed as an operator-controlled task due to the need to evaluate the zone changes for successful implementation.

6.6 SAN Fabric Security

SAN security is currently very limited in scope and features, although there is significant interest and work being done to make improvements. Security concerns for a SAN consist of unauthorized data access and unauthorized device access. These two intrusions must be secured against as thoroughly as possible, because there are many locations where security holes may appear. All configurable SAN devices, including HBAs, out-of-band management ports, and storage device consoles to name a few, are potential points for compromise of a SAN. Combinations of security schemes seem to work best and provide as many layers of protection as possible. A device approach and a SAN-wide approach should be combined into several layers of security that include both environment-specific policies and device configuration methods.

A SAN-wide approach to security is similar to a network-based security approach in an IP network. A device-based approach is similar to a host-based approach in an IP network. SAN-wide schemes are extremely limited at this time because there is currently no way to segregate connected SANs. If SAN fabrics are connected, then they become one big SAN, and if not connected, then there is no access across the gap between the SANs. So a SAN-wide security model is mostly based on policy and is not configurable into the SAN devices at this time.

A good start is a policy declaring that users accessing devices they are not authorized to use will incur dire consequences, such as having their access completely revoked. This sort of policy statement may seem like common sense, but it is useful to spell it out anyway. Because SAN-wide protections must be configured into the gateways that connect separate SANs and perhaps other devices at the edge of a SAN, it is wise to design SANs with access security in mind. When SAN-to-SAN access protection becomes available natively in SAN fabric devices, any reconfiguration required will be minimal if the SAN was originally planned with some thought given to access security. A good guess at the specific connectivity that is likely to be used when such devices are available can ease the secure deployment of SAN-to-SAN connectivity.

A device-based SAN security approach must be used to secure the SAN access points themselves, so that they cannot be compromised and used to gain further unauthorized access to the rest of the SAN. The access points for a SAN include HBAs, fabric devices, storage devices, and management consoles. Each of these devices has some sort of security or access control, and the devices should all be configured and enabled to protect SAN security. In order to enable basic security on SAN devices, a simple set of tasks can be performed. All interfaces into and out of the SAN for data transfer and management purposes should be identified for monitoring. All SAN device and host system passwords must be set using reasonable guidelines. Any available encryption method for device management access must be used. All unused SAN access ports should be disabled to prevent unauthorized devices from being attached to a SAN.

All devices, except HBAs, can be directly managed by privileged users. The privileged user accounts managing SAN devices should have "good"[7] passwords set as soon as possible after a SAN device is brought online. Any additionally available device access controls should also be enabled as soon as possible. These controls can vary from vendor to vendor of SAN devices. Access to HBA configuration is generally performed through the host system operating system, and all host system–based security rules should apply at the system level, in addition to any SAN-specific rules that have been applied to a SAN connected to the host system.

In addition to securing the SAN devices from external access, each component of a SAN must be secured from the others. Only SAN devices that must access other devices should be configured to allow that access. All other SAN device accesses should be restricted to prevent unauthorized access to an external party's data and to prevent data corruption by inadvertent accesses. Zoning of a SAN is currently most effective for providing this internal SAN access control between SAN devices. At this time, several other SAN internal access controls are being developed by industry working groups, such as the SNIA and the Fibre Channel Industry Alliance, but only zoning is currently implemented. The concepts of trusted configuration and management of SAN devices, secure SAN device addition, and encrypted SAN data are all being worked on.

Zoning can be configured with software by using WWNs or with hardware using fabric port IDs, depending on what zoning methods

---

7. See http://csrc.nist.gov for useful password and security guidelines.

the SAN fabric devices support. Each method has its own security implications. Software zoning with WWNs is susceptible to SNS (Simple Name Service) and HBA attacks based on WWN spoofing. WWN spoofing can be accomplished either by misrepresenting an HBA WWN or by forcing a WWN into a SAN zone. A successful WWN spoofing attack can be used to gain access to devices or to simply snoop traffic on the SAN. Hardware zoning is not susceptible to spoofing attacks, but it can still be compromised by the addition of a physical device to the SAN. The default behavior for most SAN fabric devices is to add a new device automatically to a SAN, and that allows additional attacks such as WWN spoofing or traffic snooping. This exposure can be limited by disabling unused ports.

Auditing all of the SAN devices can be tedious, but auditing can also be effective for detecting improper SAN access. Looking through SAN device and host system logs for events such as port logins on fabric devices, data transfers on unused fabric switch ports, or system log messages showing device resets may indicate suspicious activity. Investigation of the activity can uncover any improper access as well as help build the rule set for normal and abnormal SAN access.

Even though SAN security is currently weak at best, SAN data access can still be relatively secure. Isolation of SANs for specific user groups can help a great deal. This allows SAN deployment to go forward while limiting exposure, because all of the applications or users are owned by a single organization. Without creating too much exposure, isolation should still allow the consolidation and deployment flexibility until SAN security is sufficiently mature.

6.7 SAN Problem Diagnosis

When a problem is detected, either by the management tools used to monitor a SAN or by the failure of an application data access that should be successful but is not, the problem must be quantified and repaired. In order to diagnose problems properly, it is important to

determine the type of failure as clearly as possible. The clear classi-
fication of the failure type reduces the number of locations in the
SAN to inspect for failures or improper configurations. Start with an
examination of the logs on all of the devices in the path that the data
takes from a storage device to a host system. These logs should be
monitored continuously, but even if they are not, they will be the
best source of information on the exact nature of a SAN problem.

For example, if a host system's log reports an application error
related to a bad data access for a storage device, then the first places
to look for failures are the host system logs and the storage device
logs. Device failures and additional error messages related to the data
access failure should be recorded in these logs if there is a problem
with the host system or storage device hardware or software. If these
locations identify a problem, then it can be addressed within the host
system or storage device.

If there is no additional information in the host system or storage
device logs, then the fabric devices used for access must be examined. The logs on the fabric devices used for data access between the
host system and storage device should be checked thoroughly, and
all of the other fabric devices in the SAN should also be examined for
errors. The purpose of checking all of the fabric devices is to rule out
problems caused by device interactions. The failed components or
software in a fabric device reporting the problem may not be the root
cause of the problem.

When all of the device logs related to the data access failure have
been examined, any bad or suspect hardware should be replaced
one component at a time until the problem is repaired. If the problem is not resolved by replacing bad hardware, or if there is no hardware or software that has been reported as obviously failed, then
further analysis of the SAN and devices on it is required.

Unusual errors in device logs should be investigated thoroughly if
there appear to be no other problems or if the errors seem to be

reported often. The Fibre Channel physical specification[8] allows for a bit error rate of less than 1 bit in 10^{12} bits. Although this seems like an extremely large amount of data, it works out to less than one bit error for about every sixteen minutes of continuous data transfer. In practice, one error every hour is probably too many and should be investigated. Data transfer errors will most likely indicate a failing or poorly performing component that should be replaced. Pinpointing the suspect component in a device will still be a trial-and-error operation, because the device has not actually failed but is causing data access problems.

The components should be swapped one at a time in the order that is easiest to accomplish until the problem is fixed. A likely order for swapping devices would be Gigabit Interface Converters (GBICs) first, then cables, then host system HBAs and storage device ports. If none of the hardware replacements fix the problem, then the issue is probably in software.

Search the support information from the device vendors after completing the analysis of the devices experiencing a problem. This search can uncover any known software or hardware problems with the configuration in use in the SAN. If the support information addresses your device's behaviors and problems closely or exactly, then the likely fix will be that the documentation recommends. The recommended fix should be the first one attempted unless there is some contradictory reason for trying something else. A recommendation of a complete configuration reload should be put off while an alternate solution is investigated. A fabric switch operating system upgrade, on the other hand, is likely to help, if recommended, and should be simple to stage and implement.

Simple hardware failures are easy to repair and are likely to have little or no impact on well-built and well-designed SANs implementing

---

8. Fibre Channel Physical and Signaling Interface Specification (FC-PH) Rev. 4.3 is available at http://www.t11.org.

proper redundancy. Software and configuration failures as well as unreliable components are more difficult to discover and repair, but they are not impossible to address even in large, complex SAN implementations. A thorough step-by-step approach should be used to evaluate any SAN problem. This diagnostic method gives the shortest time to repair and the most reliable repairs.

6.8 Summary

This chapter has examined the tools and techniques for day-to-day SAN operations. Monitoring for unexpected events as well as on-going performance assessment using the methods in this chapter will ease the daily operation tasks of a SAN. The approach taken to SAN problem resolution in this chapter will also improve SAN recoverability in the event of failures.

Security concerns will also eventually become more of an issue in SANs as they are widely deployed. Being prepared to improve security on deployed SANs by designing them with future security features in mind will simplify SAN security tasks as they become necessary.

7

FUTURE SAN TECHNOLOGIES

SAN technologies are constantly changing and will continue to do so for some time. Improvements in performance and reliability are being developed for Fibre Channel as the primary SAN fabric technology of choice. Alternate SAN interconnects are being developed to provide additional SAN fabric options. Because one of the primary advantages associated with using a SAN is the increased distance that can separate a host, more long-distance SAN interconnects are rapidly being developed. Feature enhancements for SAN components are in the works, to enable better integration of the devices and the fabric to which the components are connected. The enhanced integration promises simpler deployment of data transfer features and better application awareness. Eventually, SAN storage will be configurable using virtual methods that are only loosely tied to any single physical device. The abstraction of devices through virtualized allocations will enable storage utilization improvements and more deterministic storage and systems behaviors.

7.1 SAN at a Distance

Storage interconnection technology that allows very long distances between connection endpoints, such as Fibre Channel, offers extraordinary flexibility for physical device location. Devices can be up to ten kilometers apart without using any components other than a fiber-optic cable between them. These long distances make it easier to deploy hardware because storage devices and host systems no longer have to be in close proximity.

The large distances allowed between devices on a SAN make several schemes for device deployment possible. One interesting use of the distance characteristics of a SAN is the installation of all storage devices in a single storage center with connections from many dispersed host systems running into the storage center. This scheme creates an enormous amount of resource consolidation. The storage center has only storage-specific infrastructure and becomes more manageable than a mixed-equipment data center, due to the homogeneous devices deployed in the storage center.

Another useful way to exploit the distance aspects in a SAN is to combine the resources of SAN-capable devices at more than one location without physically moving equipment. Normally, a storage device must be moved close to a host system in order to make a connection. A SAN allows connectivity between the storage device and the host system without any new infrastructure if both have links to the SAN, which means that a host system in one location can use storage space from a storage device in another location. The longer distance capability is especially useful if there is some constraint on one of the sites, such as space or power availability, that would prevent the storage device and host system from being installed at the same site.

The ten-kilometer distance limit should be more than enough to accommodate uses in most campus area and some metropolitan area environments. The flexibility that this distance provides should ease almost all deployment problems associated with the physical aspects of devices (power, space, cooling, and security). If the distance limits of the SAN are too severe to accomplish the desired goal, then there are methods that can enable even longer distances between devices on a SAN.

Dense Wavelength Division Multiplexing

In SANs using Dense Wavelength Division Multiplexing (DWDM)[1] devices, the distance between devices can be ten times greater than what Fibre Channel allows by itself. DWDM devices incur no bandwidth penalty, as long as a single unbroken optical cable can be connected between endpoints. These devices can have distances of approximately 100 kilometers between endpoints. DWDM devices also allow distances to be stretched between SAN endpoints by using multiple DWDM devices as hops between SAN endpoints. A DWDM device allows multiple data streams to travel on a single optical fiber using multiple wavelengths of light, with one connection on each wavelength in use, so the optical fiber can carry more than one connection. The multiple connections over a single optical cable make DWDM devices extremely flexible. A number of applications can make use of the even longer distances that a SAN with DWDM links can provide between devices.

Disaster recovery is one application that can take advantage of the wider SAN areas created with DWDM devices. Disaster recovery implementations generally transfer data from one site to another that is remote enough to be unaffected in the event that a catastrophe occurs at the site that contains the source data. The link between the sites is usually some kind of managed IP network link. This link generally has limited bandwidth compared with a storage I/O channel and requires protocol translation at both ends, from storage protocols to IP and back. The DWDM implementation of a disaster recovery

---

1. See the DWDM tutorial at http://www.iec.org/online/tutorials/dwdm/topic01.html.

application runs at the same speed as the native I/O channel links, and requires no protocol translation devices because the DWDM can transfer the signals unchanged through DWDM endpoints. The higher bandwidth and lack of protocol translation requirements enable better sharing of expensive long-distance cable infrastructure and better performance of the disaster recovery data transfer.

Multiple SAN data transfers can share the same DWDM link if the link is used as an ISL between SAN switch devices at the DWDM endpoints. This method enables bidirectional data transfer or data transfers from multiple systems. Bidirectional data transfer enables the two sites to be partially active and partially on standby, with each site's data being backed up at the other site. Multiple data transfers over the DWDM ISL eliminate the need for a separate link for each application requiring a disaster recovery solution. The use of the DWDM to connect components of a SAN at long distances enables fuller utilization of the link used to connect sites than a managed IP link.

SCSI over IP

Because SCSI has been organized into a group of specifications that separate physical connections from command protocols, it is possible to transfer SCSI commands over almost any transport mechanism. SCSI over IP (iSCSI) is the next logical step for connecting SANs at even greater distances than a DWDM or multiple DWDM hops can allow. Because managed IP links provide the only practical method for transferring data more than a few hundred kilometers, it is useful to transport data across a long-distance IP link directly while still using the native SCSI device access methods. The direct transport of the SCSI protocol, instead of translation of a storage protocol like Fibre Channel, reduces the workload for the devices that connect SAN components over an IP link.

Even if a long-haul link is not in use, iSCSI can still be of value if there is a heavy investment in high-speed IP networks at a site. iSCSI enables SANs to be built from traditional IP networks using Ethernet IP networks that may be more common than Fibre Channel networks, in most environments. Storage devices will eventually be able to connect to IP networks directly through some physical interface link like a Gigabit Ethernet HBA and use it to transfer data directly to iSCSI-aware host systems. This interface eliminates the need for a second dedicated high-speed storage protocol network, such as a Fibre Channel–based network, in favor of an all-IP solution.

One of the main drawbacks of the IP network solution is the high number of IP interfaces per host system needed to support sufficient I/O channels to connect to storage devices on an IP SAN. It is common to see host systems with ten or more storage I/O controllers, but it is still rather uncommon to see as many as ten physical IP interfaces on a single host system, except in the case of Web servers supporting many virtual domains at once. Using IP interfaces as I/O channels requires an enormous number of IP addresses, and even if private IP addresses[2] are used for the IP network infrastructure, SAN management will be a time-consuming task. The management and design skills needed for IP networks are more common than the skills required for Fibre Channel networks, but it is still complex and time-consuming to manage the large private IP networks that an IP Ethernet SAN using iSCSI requires.

Another problem when using iSCSI is the amount of traffic generated when data is requested from the storage devices over the IP network and then retransmitted between host systems through the same IP network. This traffic has the potential to multiply the bandwidth requirements of the IP network several times. The excess data being transferred can create problems if the IP network resources for storage devices and host systems are sharing components. Isolation of storage IP networks from host system IP networks must be carefully implemented in order to prevent bottlenecks.

---

2. See RFC 1918 for details on private IP address allocation.

Initially iSCSI can be used for very long distance data transfer needs that require a SCSI protocol. Examples include disaster recovery using block data transfer or replication using block data transfer, in which only raw data is copied when it has been changed with no awareness of how an application may be using it. These techniques are useful for last-ditch-effort data reliability and business continuance: in a disaster situation, having access to most of the data is better than having access to none of it. Disaster recovery solutions are fairly straightforward, even at long distances, but iSCSI gateway devices should eliminate the need for expensive protocol translation boxes between disaster recovery endpoints. A Fibre-Channel-to-iSCSI gateway device enables the connection of SAN components over extremely long distances with managed IP links used between the iSCSI endpoints.

The long distances that iSCSI allows for connections across networks enables the placement of host systems closer to remote users, thereby reducing application latency. Replication of a data set to remote sites using a direct storage-device-to-storage-device block data transfer over an iSCSI link allows the remote site to have a low-latency local copy of application data. This type of connectivity to remote sites creates an improved content distribution mechanism for applications with mostly read-only static data and provides a disaster recovery mechanism for the replicated data set.

iSCSI can be used to piggyback storage connectivity and services on existing IP networks. The IP networks will require upgrades to handle all of the additional data traffic, but the main advantage is that a second network infrastructure is not needed. An additional benefit of iSCSI is the simplification of management tasks, because IP is a better known entity for most administrators.

IPFC on the SAN

Having an existing Fibre Channel SAN infrastructure may make it advantageous to run host services over the SAN due to the SAN's flexible connectivity and high bandwidth availability. IP can use Fibre Channel as a link layer[3] that enables the Fibre Channel SAN to be an IP network as well. IP traffic running on a Fibre Channel network is called Internet Protocol over Fibre Channel (IPFC). The SCSI protocol traffic and the IP traffic can coexist on the SAN and may provide some interesting benefits.

The transfer of information over IP networks is a common part of many applications. Many applications transfer data among only a very small group of host systems. If, for example, these host systems are all sharing a SAN for storage consolidation purposes, then administrators may also want to take advantage of the small private IP network that can be created by running IPFC. IPFC is required because few applications are directly SAN-aware but almost all applications are IP network–aware. Overlaying an IP network on a SAN allows all IP services to be run, with the potential to increase data transfer performance significantly compared with an IP network based on traditional, inherently lower performance Ethernet technologies.

Private IP networks for specific applications are common for backups, NFS traffic, and other high-priority application traffic where a network with better and more deterministic performance is required. If you have a group of host systems that need to exchange data in order to run an application and are using SAN storage, you may also find that using the SAN for application-specific data traffic via IPFC provides significant benefits. A private IP address range should be used, but no routing can be implemented because there are currently no gateways that support Fibre Channel connectivity to any other link layer. If these conditions are acceptable, then a SAN can support a private IPFC network for expedited application traffic without problems.

The potential drawbacks involve performance and management. Performance requirements on the SAN are increased if IP and storage

---

3. See http://webopedia.internet.com/quick_ref/OSI_Layers.html for a brief explanation of network layers.

traffic are used on the same physical network. Typically these re-quirements are not a problem because most Ethernet-based LANs are currently using 10Mbps or 100Mbps link speeds. The required bandwidth is between 1 and 10 percent of the overall SAN Fibre Channel link speed of 1Gbps, so there is plenty of overhead for the IP traffic even on a heavily utilized SAN. At the moment, all current IPFC implementations are proprietary because the specification is a draft standard; it should be ratified sometime in 2002. This lack of a completed standard has the potential to create management prob-lems with compatibility of HBAs and fabric devices. The devices all have to communicate together but have differing and incompatible implementation methods. A homogeneous approach to selecting an HBA vendor lessens the problems a bit, but a truly general imple-mentation requires the finalization of a good standard.

7.2 Scalability

SANs and the devices they are built from are fairly new, having only been widely available since 1999. As the technologies and methods mature, SANs will become more scalable. Faster fabric devices with higher numbers of ports and more features are constantly being developed. New technologies and techniques are being invented all the time to improve SAN performance and scalability.

SAN performance increases in the near term can be gained mainly in Fibre Channel improvements and better switching methods. Improvements to Fibre Channel will enable more traffic to move through fabric devices by increasing bandwidth. Better switching will allow more frames to be moved through the fabric devices with better determination of traffic priorities on the SAN.

SAN scalability is being improved by increasing the number of ports in a single fabric device and by simplifying the management of all devices on the SAN. More ports are an obvious scalability improvement, due to the additional connectivity the ports provide, but they also help ease the management of high-port-count SANs by consolidating more ports behind a single, manageable front end in a single device. Other SAN devices will see improved management over time as device-specific standards are generalized and finalized. SAN management standards will enable SAN control from any authorized SAN entry point, including fabric switches, storage devices, and host systems, because there will be a unified way for all potential management devices to address any device on the SAN.

Fabric Performance Increases

SAN fabric performance will be directly driven by Fibre Channel improvements until some other interconnect replaces Fibre Channel as the medium of choice for SANs. SAN fabrics are all currently based on 1Gbps links with 2Gbps Fibre Channel in initial deployment. 2Gbps Fibre Channel became available at the end of 2001 on many SAN-aware devices.

The next step for Fibre Channel will be speed improvements to 4Gbps or 10Gbps. The work being done to accomplish 10Gbps Fibre Channel is proceeding at about the same pace as the 4Gbps effort, so it is likely that 4Gbps will be bypassed. The likely arrival of 10Gbps speeds will occur sometime in late 2003. Wide adoption of 10Gbps Fibre Channel may take a year or more.

Another expected fabric performance increase related to Fibre Channel will come from improving switching methods to accommodate different classes of traffic. Today, all Fibre Channel traffic is treated equally or uses gross quality of service controls when being transferred. The Fibre Channel quality of service specification is currently being improved to create a more deterministic way to control data transfers in a SAN. As better quality of service methods are implemented in fabric devices, the devices will become more efficient in the delivery of data. Performance will increase as switch efficiency increases, due to less waste in switch overhead when trying to ensure proper delivery of high-priority data.

Fabric implementations are being studied and improved constantly. HBAs are being improved to provide more on-board processing to replace host system processing, which will improve throughput. Fabric topologies are constantly reevaluated to provide the best possible availability and performance. Storage devices are being modified to take advantage of SAN features that improve speed, simplify data transfers, and extend data access to more distant endpoints.

Storage Feature Enhancements

As storage devices are deployed in a SAN environment, access methods and behaviors will change. More host systems will have access to individual storage devices, which drives utilization of the storage devices up, giving a better return on storage investment. Storage devices will also be able to take advantage of the improved flexibility and performance of SANs by implementing new storage features and improving existing features.

Storage devices will begin to implement features with SAN connectivity in mind. One likely change in storage devices will be the use of the distances that Fibre Channel allows to separate components of the storage device. The disks can be separated from the storage processors and caches, making the storage devices more modular. Caching devices will even be completely uncoupled from disk devices while still providing access to the disks. This separation will allow any amount of storage to be connected at any point in the SAN while still providing low-latency access for host systems through the cache devices to commonly accessed data. Storage can then be accessed in the best possible way for the application, whether or not it is cache-hostile, by choosing whether or not to access storage through a SAN cache appliance.

As the flexibility of SANs is explored, storage devices will also become more configurable, with the storage devices themselves virtually becoming small SANs internally, with connections to external SANs. The ability to modify the storage devices internally relies on the same mechanisms that are used externally to modify the SAN. Storage devices will become self-contained networks of devices with several external connections that provide storage services. Storage devices will also become much more modular, so that a feature can be added or removed by physically changing the configuration of the storage device.

Storage devices will also internalize services that are now provided by external devices. Data sharing, data transfers, and application data integrity will be handled by the storage device in order to reduce the number of steps required to move data between devices. The reduction of data movement will improve performance of the storage system as a whole by reducing the number of I/O operations performed when changes occur or data is moved.

Storage device performance increases will also come from improved components. Disk drives and device interconnects will get faster as storage processors become more efficient at optimizing application-specific data access. Storage processors will improve data access evaluation to go beyond simple sequential access detection and read-ahead caching to subtle application access pattern optimization that is also application-aware. Storage processors will be able to analyze I/O demand and be able to modify work modes based on past and expected I/O demands in a proactive way that complements subtle application behaviors. The application awareness will enable the storage devices to predict what the next most likely data access will be, improving data access performance. Storage processors are also likely to perform metadata operations for application data integrity as well as data sharing and replication.

Features in storage devices will be updated to take advantage of the SAN as well. Remote data replication for disaster recovery is beginning to move from proprietary links and protocols to generic fabric-based infrastructure such as Fibre Channel and DWDM links. SAN connectivity makes it possible for one-to-one remote data replications to become a fanout from one source to multiple targets for multiple purposes. This becomes possible on a SAN because storage devices can now use a single port to see multiple devices instead of just the one device at the other end of the cable.

Storage device–based snapshots become much more useful in a SAN environment due to the improved connectivity. A storage device is no longer limited by the number of ports it has for connectivity to host system HBAs. This freedom makes snapshot data set copies in a storage device extremely distributable for concurrent uses such as backups, development, and testing without running out of connectivity. Only absolute storage device performance is the limiting factor.

7.3 SAN/Application Integration

SANs will eventually become an operational part of applications. As more SANs are deployed, applications will become SAN-aware in the same way that applications have become host system cluster–aware. SAN-aware applications will be able to make use of the SAN connectivity and features in order to improve availability and performance.

Backup applications will be the first to benefit from being truly SAN-aware. The ability to dynamically add and remove backup devices from hosts will enable backup systems to do away with device servers and backup IP networks. A SAN connection to the backup device or separate backup SAN will be all that is required to perform data backups. The backup server will need only to reallocate the SAN backup devices and initiate a backup job on the host system. The backup will then run as if the backup devices were local to the host system running the job until the job is complete. The backup devices will be reallocated to the next host system needing to be backed up. The backup application will need to understand only the SAN zoning method for the backup to be accomplished.

Data sharing is another application that will be improved by direct awareness of the SAN. Performance will be the main improvement for data sharing over the SAN. Data sharing with a SAN can be accomplished today with a variety of software tools, but they all require an IP network as a component of the application. Native SAN-only data sharing will remove the reliance on the IP network and data-sharing protocols such as NFS. It is expected that the SAN data-sharing mechanisms will improve upon existing data-sharing protocols and that they will also make efficient use of the high-speed SAN links. This should provide performance improvements over an IP network–based data-sharing solution.

SANs will also provide improved data replication through application integration with the SAN and SAN appliances. A SAN appliance is any hardware device connected to the SAN with a single dedicated function, such as data replication or heterogeneous storage device mirroring. Applications can be developed to access multiple versions of the same data set. The replication of data will be handled by dedicated SAN devices, which create an abstract access method for any arbitrary storage device that a host system accesses. The access of storage devices through an abstraction method will enable host systems to use all storage devices on a SAN, as if they were a single generic type. The SAN appliance will also have the ability to create multiple copies of the data stream for replication of data on differing storage devices without host system involvement. This ability will greatly reduce the problems of data replication for applications that do not have a built-in mechanism.

Database applications can also take advantage of SAN features in addition to simply using SAN storage for the database host systems. As database applications become more parallel, the accesses to SAN storage devices in parallel will have some benefits. The manual process of tuning the application by shuffling data from hot spots can become automatic as applications that are SAN-aware become self-tuning for storage performance. A continuous assessment of the SAN fabric device and storage device utilization will allow intelligent applications to recommend or automatically invoke storage or SAN changes for tuning purposes. Applications will be able to migrate data from an overutilized storage device or route traffic to an alternate path before a performance problem occurs, if fabric device utilization threshold rules are exceeded.

Application integration with a SAN will enable new ways to deploy storage in support of applications. SANs will enable applications to migrate data efficiently, to their best advantage, without requiring more than the standard set of SAN interfaces. The features a SAN provides to applications will have enormous benefits for deployment and storage usage efficiencies.

7.4 Storage Virtualization

Having many devices attached to a SAN has the potential to create serious management issues if there are many different types of devices as well as different configuration and management methods. Because the number of device vendors for SANs is unlikely to be reduced to a manageable number, the idea of storage virtualization has been developed. Storage virtualization allows any storage device to be deployed in any way on any host system. No matter what the interior configuration of the device, it will be deployable by any combination of storage size, storage performance, or availability requirements, if the requirements are physically within the device's characteristics.

In the simplest case, a specific storage size can be allocated from any storage device, or combination of storage devices, that has the amount of free space required. A host system that needs 500GB of storage space can have the space allocated from three different storage devices from three different manufacturers. The allocation can be 100GB from device A, 150GB from device B, and 250GB from device C without the host system being aware of it or having to perform different management and configuration tasks on the different storage devices. This allocation is handled by the storage virtualization engine. The ability to allocate storage from multiple devices will dramatically improve utilization.

The real benefit of storage virtualization comes from applying performance and availability rules to allocated storage space. Eventually a request for 500GB will also give the administrator allocating the space the option of specifying IOPS, bandwidth, and alternate path requirements. The requirements will also be specified as best-effort requests or demands that must be met for storage to be successfully allocated. The combination of these performance and availability characteristics will make storage deployment simpler, more effective, and more efficient.

A request for 500GB with a best effort at 10,000 IOPS and a must-have requirement of two paths to the storage devices will create much more deterministic deployment of storage. Storage virtualization parameter settings will also allow for better assessment of storage device and SAN device performance and utilization, because there will be a baseline set of expectations to compare with observed results.

The exact mechanisms for storage virtualization are not yet completely determined, but there are several currently available software and hardware solutions with limited functionality. Both the software and hardware storage virtualization engines rely on a virtualization server to control access to storage devices. This access control requires that the storage devices be set up before they can be used. In the future the virtualization server will configure the storage devices and then, using SAN zoning, present the newly configured storage space to the target host system.

Current storage virtualization engines provide the ability only to allocate storage from certain storage devices without implementing the quality of service or availability features that will be required for true virtualized storage. These storage virtualization engines are a good start, but they are incomplete. Eventually all storage devices will be addressable by virtualization engines. The storage virtualization engines will have known limits for storage device performance parameters, so that the quality of service requests can be reliably assessed and allocated out of the existing SAN storage device resources. This set of known information about the storage devices will prevent virtualization engines from oversubscribing storage or SAN resources.

Virtualization engines for a SAN will need to be deployed in the appropriate location on a SAN to be of maximum use. That location is being actively debated; there will likely be several good solutions. Figure 7.1 shows how storage is managed and virtualized in systems with directly attached storage today, and where storage resources might be virtualized on a SAN in the future. Host systems need to be made aware of the storage virtualization by installing an operating system driver to communicate with the SAN virtualization components, if the operating system or volume managers are not virtual storage–aware. Some combination of the virtualization components in several locations will probably be the best choice.

Unifying the storage allocation methods and still achieving the performance requirements of the applications using the SAN, without specific knowledge of individual storage devices, will reduce the amount of time and effort spent deploying storage. It will eventually be sufficient simply to provide connectivity, and the storage virtualization engine will take care of the allocation details based on whatever rule set is defined.

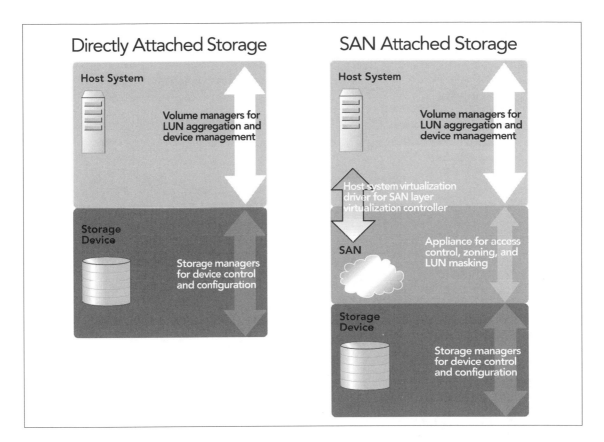

FIGURE 7.1

Storage virtualization locations for directly attached storage and SAN storage

7.5 Summary

While the exact future of SAN technologies is still quite uncertain, this chapter offered a brief discussion of the most likely directions for SANs. The technologies in this chapter are beginning to be used in applications because they are so compelling, even though the final standards for most of them are not complete. The use of new technologies in SANs—a somewhat new technology itself—can provide solutions to many long-standing storage problems.

REFERENCES

BOOKS

Ancot Corporation. *Basics of SCSI*. Fourth Edition. Menlo Park, Calif.: Ancot Corporation, 1998.

Ancot Corporation. *What Is Fibre Channel?* Fifth Edition. Menlo Park, Calif.: Ancot Corporation, 2000.

Benner, Alan F. *Fibre Channel*. New York: McGraw-Hill, 1996.

Clark, Tom. *Designing Storage Area Networks*. Reading, Mass.: Addison-Wesley, 1999.

Gunther, Neil J. *The Practical Performance Analyst*. New York: McGraw-Hill, 1998.

WEB SITES

www.dmtf.org—Distributed Management Task Force, Inc.

www.fibrechannel.com—Fibre Channel Industry Association

www.snia.org—Storage Networking Industry Association

www.t11.org—International Committee for Information Technology Standards, T11 Fibre Channel Technical Committee

ACRONYMS

CIFS	Common Internet File System
DAS	direct-attached storage
DWDM	Dense Wavelength Division Multiplexing
ETL	extraction, transformation, and load
FC-SCSI	Fibre Channel–SCSI
FSPF	Fibre Channel Shortest Path First
GBICs	Gigabit Interface Converters
HBA	host bus adapter
IOPS	I/O operations per second
IPFC	Internet Protocol over Fibre Channel
iSCSI	SCSI over IP
ISL	InterSwitch Link
JBOD	Just-a-Bunch-of-Disks
LUN	logical unit number
MIB	Management Information Base
NAS	network-attached storage
NFS	Network File System
OLTP	on-line transaction processing
QoS	Quality of Service
RDBMS	relational database management system
SMB	Server Message Block
SNIA	Storage Network Industry Association
SNMP	Simple Network Management Protocol
SNS	Simple Name Server
WWN	world-wide name

INDEX

A

acccss

control

of multipath port fanout, LUN issues, 122

of SAN devices, 154

virtualization server reliance on, 173

DAS

characteristics (table), 19

conversion to SAN fabric storage access, 105

data

evaluation improvements in future storage devices, 169

as SAN application, 12

scalability of, snapshot data copy use, 88

through IP network, as storage solution, 18

LUN, control, 121

multipath, as core zone issue, 120

NAS

characteristics (table), 19

NFS as protocol for, 18

points, device-based security approach to, 153

random, percentage of, as I/O pattern, 36

SAN

characteristics (table), 19

fabric as mechanism for, 18

sequential, percentage of, as I/O pattern, 36

storage, SAN advantages over NAS, 3

unauthorized, as SAN security concern, 152

addresses/addressing

device, as SAN operating system selection factor, 85

IP, private, RFC 1918 as information source for, (footnote), 163

advantages

of multipath SAN nature, 1

agents

host system, SNMP information reporting, 134

in-band, 136

SNMP, information gathering and configuration management by, 133

allocation

device

fabric reconfiguration use for, 151

tools for managing, 27

LUN, 118

resource, selection factors for a special purpose device for, 84

storage, SAN improvement of, 13

analysis

application

I/O characteristics, 58

I/O issues, role in SAN design and deployment, 32

importance for SAN selection, 20

measurement simulation, 127

181

informIT

YOUR GUIDE TO IT REFERENCE

Articles

Keep your edge with thousands of free articles, in-depth features, interviews, and IT reference recommendations – all written by experts you know and trust.

Online Books

Answers in an instant from **InformIT Online Book's** 600+ fully searchable on line books. For a limited time, you can get your first 14 days **free**.

Catalog

Review online sample chapters, author biographies and customer rankings and choose exactly the right book from a selection of over 5,000 titles.

Register
Your Book

at www.awprofessional.com/register

You may be eligible to receive:

- Advance notice of forthcoming editions of the book
- Related book recommendations
- Chapter excerpts and supplements of forthcoming titles
- Information about special contests and promotions throughout the year
- Notices and reminders about author appearances, tradeshows, and online chats with special guests

Contact us

If you are interested in writing a book or reviewing manuscripts prior to publication, please write to us at:

Editorial Department
Addison-Wesley Professional
75 Arlington Street, Suite 300
Boston, MA 02116 USA
Email: AWPro@aw.com

Addison-Wesley

Visit us on the Web: http://www.awprofessional.com